STAGE
FIGHT

Stage Fight: How to Punch Your Fears of Public Speaking In the Face! / By Cody Smith

Paperback Edition ISBN-13: 978-0-9996942-0-6

Paperback Edition ISBN-10: 0-9996942-0-0

Kindle Edition ISBN-13: 978-0-9996942-1-3

Kindle Edition ISBN-10: 0-9996942-1-9

Library of Congress Control Number: 2017919726

Published by Nelaco Press

Printed in the USA

DEDICATION

To my wife and daughter.

*Words will never suffice to describe my love for you both.
My life is forever blessed to be a part of yours.*

TABLE OF CONTENTS

FOREWORD BY PATRICK KING

Public speaking is unlike many other fears that exist in our daily lives.

We know it's essentially harmless, and yet we do more to avoid it than almost anything. We know we're prepared, but we can't shake the inevitable anxiety. We might even feel confident, but we can never escape that little voice inside our heads that says, "But what if . . . ?"

Are the people we admire on stage simply born with it and barely the same species as us? It might seem that way, but that's as disempowering a belief as any. That's surely not the reason you decided to open this book, is it?

To that end, I enthusiastically recommend Cody's book Stage Fight. We have similar stories in being decidedly ungifted at public speaking, experiencing failure, then dissecting the elements that matter.

Many people will tell you the importance of public speaking, but you don't need to be convinced by that. Cody's book is chock-full of the *hows* that will get you from your Point A to your Point B, whatever they may be.

Patrick King

Patrickkingconsulting.com

INTRODUCTION

Public speaking is scary. Period. There aren't many venues out there requiring you to be completely vulnerable. Every mistake you make is public knowledge, recorded in the minds of your audience. Every fumble, mumble, and stutter could bring judgement.

If we make a mistake on stage, the impact is far greater than making a mistake from the comfort of our couch, in our office cubicle, or around close friends and family. In front of a crowd, we amplify the consequences of completely sucking at something as simple as speaking.

Thus, we build mental barriers to filter out any reason or opportunity to develop public speaking skills. We view those opportunities as threats to our lifestyle, to our comfort, to our current status quo. We avoid these opportunities at all costs.

When our teacher pushes the deadline for the class presentation or our boss cancels that big brief, we react as if a jury deemed us "not guilty." A sigh of relief fills every crevice of our being, ending with an even bigger exhale while saying, "Oh thank God." The sun shines once again, and we can go back to the way things were. The way things "should" be within our own sphere of comfort.

If you're sick and tired of feeling like you just can't get a grip over yourself in front of an audience, or you wish the days leading up to a speaking engagement weren't filled with dread and fear, then let this book guide you to change that.

Maybe your past experiences with public speaking could be summed up in two words: stage fright. I want you to know I've been there. I struggled for years to speak confidently front and center.

It all started with a terrible performance in middle school. I carried that memory with me and re-lived it every time I had to speak to a crowd thereafter.

Every second on a stage of any kind felt like suffering. I dreaded staring into the eyes of my audience, and I couldn't understand why it was so hard for me. I was literally afraid to say words— words! I responded as if someone were holding a gun to my head.

Now I can address a crowd confidently. However, I want to be very transparent with you: I am not a professional speaker. I don't have 20 years' experience as a public speaker. I've never been paid to speak. Nor have I ever given a keynote speech. While I hope to have these experiences one day, I can't list them on my current resume.

What I can say is that following the steps and exercises laid out in this book changed me and they can change you, too. Before I was someone who would rather be the guy in the casket vs the poor soul who had to give the eulogy. Following what's in the chapters to come helped me become someone who could pitch a business idea in college and raise over $17k to turn that idea into reality.

Without overcoming my fears of public speaking, I would never have been able to do that. Overcoming my fears also raised my confidence through the roof. I don't dread having to speak anymore. I look forward to speaking.

I want that same result for you. I want you to walk out on stage standing tall and confident. I want to see you conquer your fears of public speaking.

I promise you here and now if you read and implement the steps found in this book, you WILL become a courageous speaker—in fact, it's impossible to not become one after you do so.

To start, you must decide whether you want to become a confident, courageous speaker by reading this book, or if you want to continue in fear and cast this book aside. You get to choose whether your life will be one big stage *fright* or whether you will own it, making it your very own stage *fight*.

Get ready to conquer your fears of public speaking by taking action today and choosing to read this book to become a confident, courageous speaker.

Welcome to the Stage Fight Club where we punch our fears IN. THE. FACE. Read on.

SECTION 1

—

MY STORY

CHAPTER 1

WHERE IT ALL BEGAN

Sitting in Ms. Dory's (not her real name) English class in 6th grade, I remember holding my stomach when she announced it was time to begin our product presentations.

We had known for weeks we had to present a new product for purchase, complete with an original jingle—since no product is complete without a silly tune to get stuck in the heads of potential customers.

But when Ms. Dory announced three weeks prior we would have to present to the rest of the class, I did the only logical thing I think anyone in my situation would do: I pushed off working on my presentation until the last minute, which meant the night before it was due.

I waited for a miracle to save me from what was to come, hoping the day before Ms. Dory would remind the class to have their presentations ready by tomorrow, but then say, "Except Cody. You will not have to present tomorrow, and you will still get an A." That, of course, did not happen.

The stars of mercy did not align that day.

Instead, my teacher not only reminded the class to have everything ready for the next day, she looked at me and asked, "Cody, you're going to have everything ready for tomorrow, right?"

I can only assume my demeanor changed, perhaps my jaw dropped, and that is why she picked me out. I probably gave a not so reassuring nod as Ms. Dory responded with a reluctant, "I hope so."

My gut hit the floor. *Crap, she knows!* Previous Cody had just screwed over present Cody. It was an easy decision to ignore the assignment, put off the feared public speaking, and let future Cody deal with it. Well, future Cody was now present Cody, and present Cody was pissed at himself!

The bell rang, and I remembered to breathe. The rest of the day I dreaded every passing moment. Every second brought me closer to the moment I had been running away from for the past three weeks.

One would think as soon as I got home, I would immediately get to work on my presentation—that did not happen. Once again I did whatever I could to distract myself from any thoughts of speaking in front of my class, continuing to shoot myself in the foot, but I was running out of feet to shoot.

It wasn't until after dinner that I finally told my parents I needed a poster board for my presentation due the next day.

They were far from stoked to run to the store to grab supplies for the assignment I'd known about for three weeks.

After receiving the supplies and a lecture from my parents on procrastination, I frantically wrote a description of my product on my poster board. My product was a baseball that would go in any direction you wanted after you threw it. A million-dollar idea—I know.

We had to draw a picture of our product, so I thought I would draw a baseball flying through the air. Unfortunately, I sucked at drawing, and I still do to this day. It ended up looking like one of those Furby toys from the 90s but on fire. Not exactly what I was going for.

With the drawing "done" it was time to work on that stupid jingle. I figured a jingle was similar to *Twinkle Twinkle Little Star* or *Jingle Bells* since "jingle" was in the title. I also assumed the jingle had to be just as long as a song.

I put the finishing touches on my poster board, rolled it up, and stuck it in my backpack. I went straight to bed, not looking forward to the next day, hoping to avoid destiny.

Destiny did not slide her plans across my desk for my approval. I would have vetoed the crap out of what she had in store for me tomorrow.

This brings me to where this story started: the morning of presentations. I was sitting at my desk, holding my stomach, and praying my name would not be called first. Luckily, we went in alphabetical order. My last name starts with an "S," which extended my wait for electric-chair-like torture.

Ms. Dory asked for volunteers to go first. To me, that was like signing up for a suicide mission. My best friend, who sat beside me, raised his hand and volunteered as tribute. He had a mother and father who loved him, and he had the audacity to smile about going first. Keep in mind I was homeschooled up until 6th grade which made a lot of things foreign to me.

Wanting to go first made sense when lining up to go to lunch on fried chicken Wednesdays or being picked first when deciding kickball teams during P.E. But this—this was insanity.

My friend made his way to the front of the class, propped up his poster board and presented his product. His product just so happened to be a baseball bat that guaranteed home runs. He glided through his presentation like he was enjoying it, and then he concluded with the required ending: the jingle.

He chimed, "Whoop, there it is. Whoop, there it is."

Eight words. Eight words and he was done. The class applauded, which was common courtesy for each student.

Taking his seat, he whispered to me with a grin, "Glad that's over." It was at that moment I finally understood what a jingle was. In comparison, I wrote a freaking song!

Students one by one went up, presented their product, jingled for a few seconds, and completed their trial. I tried to quickly think how to shorten and make it jingle-ish. But I was so afraid to give my presentation that I could not think straight let alone focus. I wanted to be brave like my friend who volunteered, but every time I had the chance, I got scared, froze, and did nothing as I waited for my turn.

Finally, my name was called, and I gave the signal for my body to move out from my desk and up to the front. Nothing happened.

Nothing happened for a good 10 seconds, which is long enough for even the most carefree students to look in my direction and wonder what's up.

I sat there as if my brain needed to reboot after a "blue screen of death" episode. I eventually managed to grab my poster and walk in front of the whole class. Propping up my poster board, I turned to face everyone. With everyone staring at me, I felt like I couldn't breathe.

At that moment, everyone expected words to come out of my mouth. Instead, I think I just held my mouth open for the whole class to see. I'm sure it was impressive.

I swallowed and began to fumble through my speech. Realizing I had not practiced, not once, I turned back to my poster to read off the stats of my super baseball, but I had written in pencil. Pencil that I could hardly read standing right next to my poster board. I was going to have to wing it, which wasn't far off from what I was doing anyway.

I just started pointing at my board, making stuff up, and trying to describe what my product could do with my hands, which just confused my classmates. I was choking on almost every word leading up to the grand finale: the jingle.

I made an instant decision to take the first line of my song and the last, and spit it out. Hindsight is always 20/20. I should have at least come up with a tune for my song, but I had to wing that, also.

It did not go well. *Twinkle Twinkle Little Star* was the first tune (go figure) that came to mind. After I finished, the class stared at me like a deer in the headlights. Silence speaks for itself. I did not do well.

After a long silence, the teacher started clapping and slowly the rest of the class followed. It was hard to cut through the awkwardness walking back to my desk. My friend looked at me and said, "Good job." Those words floated right past me as I sat there trying to make sense out of what just happened.

I felt awful and judged, mainly because I kept judging myself over my terrible performance. Hosting my own pity party, I compared myself to the other students who seemed to have no problem speaking in front of the class.

It was finally over, but it didn't feel over. Fear was simply replaced with complete and utter embarrassment. I was ashamed, and I never wanted to feel that way again. Unfortunately, history has a way of repeating itself. . . .

CHAPTER 2

HISTORY REPEATS ITSELF

My experience giving a presentation in 6th grade haunted me whenever I had to speak in front of any crowd thereafter, even affecting my ability to ask or answer questions in class.

I would remember and relive the fear, the mistakes, and the embarrassment. Fearing the same tragedy over and over again, I was a broken record constantly repeating the same broken song.

Through middle school and high school, I did whatever I could to avoid speaking in public. That mindset started affecting other aspects of my life. As much as I wanted to take the lead role (or any role) in drama class, I just couldn't risk screwing up again.

Church was equally terrifying. Being asked to read scriptures out loud was bad enough. Having to pray over our Sunday School class was even worse. Having God in the audience added even more pressure. He is the big cheese after all.

I believed avoiding my fears was the best route. Keeping it deep within me, I held it close and without fail reminded myself consistently, as if it were a sacred family creed.

What I did not realize is that that belief was a limiting belief. It gave me boundaries that I dared not cross. Those boundaries and limitations were not even real, and sadly, I was the one who put them there.

I kept telling myself that same old story: "I am terrible at speaking, nothing good can come from it, and my audience will think I'm an idiot."

That vision was not serving me. It was crippling me. You tell yourself a lie long enough, and you'll start to believe it, even obsess over it.

It was time to start a new story. A remix if you please. Half way through high school, I got fed up with sucking. I wondered why some people had no trouble speaking in front of the class when other students, myself included, were terrified. I started taking notes and studying what some students did well and what other students did poorly.

The students who performed really well seemed at ease or comfortable to speak in front of the class. To them, it just didn't seem to be a big deal. However, the students who were afraid, fearing a very real consequence if they performed poorly, spoke with less confidence.

From that observation alone, I could not determine any tips or strategies to help me out. The only thing I could conclude was that some students were good at it and some were not. That did not give me any hope, but I wasn't ready to give up just yet. I would have to look elsewhere.

At some point early in my 10th-grade year in high school, I decided to do something drastic: buy a book on public speaking and actually read it. Crazy idea, right??

Keep in mind my idea of books was something adults bought to decorate a shelf filled with other books.

I didn't have a job nor could I drive at the time. I gathered up what money I had left from my birthday and Christmas, and I asked my dad to take me to Books-A-Million. My dad loves Books-A-Million, so it was pretty easy convincing him to take me there.

Up until that point, I had only gone there when I was seven to trade Pokémon cards with other kids. Going in to actually buy books was new and kind of exciting.

I made my way over to a self-help section, eventually finding a section on public speaking. Of the choices, I narrowed my purchase down to two books. I'd like to say I chose them due to their superior content, but I picked those two simply because they were cheaper.

I wasn't a zealous reader at the time, but I was committed to reading those books from cover to cover to learn whatever I could to become a better speaker. In those books were secrets I could uncover—or so I thought.

One book focused on the structure, the skeleton of the presentation. Without that, your message could not stand on its own.

I thought *well this is it!* This is what I needed all along. I was missing a clear and concise structure to my message. How could I expect to do well without a well-thought-out message? Of course,

I was afraid to speak without a properly structured speech, who wouldn't be? I believed this was the answer to my problem.

The second book concentrated on keeping the audience's attention throughout, giving several tactics.

I figured by applying this advice, I was golden. I wasn't the problem after all. My message and engagement were the root cause of all public speaking evil, and I had the tools to fix it.

I truly thought my suffering was over, but I would soon find out that my newly-discovered knowledge was just addressing the symptoms and not the cause.

CHAPTER 3

ROOT CAUSE

Not long after reading those two books, I had to give a presentation in biology class on the plant cell. I formed my presentation like the first book suggested to create order and clarity. I had a clear beginning, middle, and end. Then I planned a few things to keep the attention of my classmates.

I felt better with my presentation in check. Sitting at my desk, I knew I was prepared, but that did not stop my thoughts from running back to all the times when I screwed up. All the way back to that terrible day in middle school.

The fear started taking control and settling in like an old friend.

My name was eventually called, and this presentation started and ended like all the rest. The well-thought-out structure of my speech was riddled with awkward mumblings while I constantly repeated myself. I filled every silence with an audible noise like 'um' and 'uh' because I just couldn't handle the silence.

If you were wondering if I kept my classmates' attention—I absolutely did, but not because I expertly executed the techniques in the second book. I was a train wreck and my audience couldn't look away. I asked questions to the class that no one answered. The silence destroyed me, a stinging reject unlike what I had experienced before.

I even tried to tell a joke, which apparently didn't have a punchline, so no one laughed. Take it from me. Jokes about plant cells: just don't.

I did not understand. I followed what the book suggested, but as soon as I got in front of my class, I flopped. It was as if I personally recorded my past failures, rewound the tape, and pressed play.

I went on with my life accepting this was just how things were going to turn out no matter how hard I tried. Months would go by before finally fate would give me . . .

CHAPTER 4

AN UNLIKELY SOURCE OF HOPE

My endeavor to be a greater speaker took almost a year hiatus before something sparked my interest once again. This spark came from a very unlikely source: someone who was just as terrified to speak in front of people.

In 11th grade I took an elective class. Halfway through the semester, we participated in mock interviews in front of three students acting like potential employers.

I was nervous, but it was literally just three other classmates across a table. I got through my interview without a panic attack. It didn't really feel like speaking to a crowd since I was just answering questions.

Another student, Jessica (not her real name), was up next. Two other classmates and I interviewed her, asking typical interview questions:

"What experience do you have working?"

"Describe a time you solved a problem?"

"What is your greatest weakness?"

Early in the interview, Jessica's hands and voice started shaking uncontrollably. She was completely overwhelmed to speak in front of only three of her peers during an interview that amounted to nothing. Not even a grade.

I stopped asking questions while the other two students finished up what questions we had left.

I just watched her. Creep factor aside, it was like seeing myself from outside looking in. I realized that's exactly how I feel in front of a crowd. If that interview had lasted any longer, I'm sure she would have started to cry.

After all the interviews had finished and before class ended, I asked Jessica if she was all right. She assured me she was, and we began discussing our public speaking fears. What she said next made me rethink how I tried approaching my inability to speak in public: "I don't know why I get so nervous. I get so worked up over the littlest things. If I could just control my fear, I could act normal in front of people."

"Yeah, I know I wish . . ." The bell rang and what she said really hit me like a ton of bricks.

The problem was clear: I had zero control over my fears. None. I tried controlling the structure of my speech or keeping my audience's attention. But external solutions were not the answer to my problem.

The real problem was I did not know how to attack my fear head-on. Up until that point I believed if I was afraid of something, then I could not do anything about it.

Never had I thought to approach my problem from the viewpoint of controlling my fears. I figured they were here to stay. I really wasn't sure how to control what I was afraid of, but I was excited to find out.

I had faced my fears before, but public speaking seemed like a humongous hurdle compared to everything else. When it came to riding a roller coaster for the first time, I, at least, had friends and family with me. Shoot, even when I was little and afraid of the dark, I had my mom or dad or one of my brothers with me.

Speaking was a solo act for the most part. The fear doesn't feel the same. Asking girls out was even easier than speaking to a crowd of people. Either way, I had felt a sprinkle of hope that things could change.

Immediately after school, I went to the family computer and typed into Google "how to control my fears." The next two hours (before my parents eventually kicked me off) was information overload. Most of what I read was vanilla, but there was some useful advice. I found books, TED talks, and even YouTube channels dedicated to helping people overcome their fears.

By taking what I've learned, applying those lessons to public speaking, and added my own methods, I've become a courageous speaker. I've included the lessons in the following chapters along with stories of my experience successfully applying them.

We are going to get into the nitty-gritty of our fear of speaking, how to deal with our fears, and how to punch our fears in the face each and every time we step onto a stage wherever and whenever that might be.

—Cody's Note—

If you illegally downloaded my book, then I'll show you how to do all of that for free! Let's face it: I can't stop you if you do so enjoy the ride.

Are you with me? Great. Let's get started with the first thing you need to address: yourself.

SECTION 2

—

UNDERSTANDING AND CHANGING YOUR PERSPECTIVE OF FEAR

CHAPTER 5

YOUR WORST ENEMY

You are your worst enemy. Period. Thus, the biggest obstacle you will have to overcome is yourself. The first person to let you down is yourself. The first person to tell you that you can't do something is you.

I'm going to get pretty personal so hang with me. Starting today you need to take responsibility for your life. If you don't, you will simply take shelter behind the walls of your comfort, pointing your finger at the world, blaming others for everything that goes wrong in your life.

While acting like the victim is playing it "safe," this type of safety does not benefit you. Playing the victim will not give you what you want in life. Playing the victim will not push you in the direction towards success. No. This "safety" is simply a convenient crutch.

We use it like a shield to hide behind to "protect" us from feeling vulnerable, uncomfortable, or afraid. But this shield only protects and keeps us "safe" from our greater selves. The person we want to be. The person we can become.

Trust me, I know this all too well. I've held up that same shield more times than I'd ever like to admit. I've hidden behind my sphere of comfort as if I were doing myself a favor. But in reality, I was shooting myself in the foot by preventing myself from growing, reaching my greatness, and becoming the person I had no idea I could be.

Do you really want to hold on to the victim identity? Is that truly the life you would choose for yourself? The old you might have, but since you are reading this book, I believe the present you is probably sick and tired of the old you.

Leave the old you behind.

You might be a little angry at yourself for letting it go on for as long as it has. That's okay. That's good actually. That's the new you cracking through that old skin you wore for too long.

You're about ready to toss that shield aside and pick up a sword you should have been holding this whole time, but you just weren't ready to see it.

You have to grip this sword with both hands fully committed, which means casting your shield aside and your insecurities with it. That's good because you won't need it anymore.

You're about to fight the hardest opponent you will ever trade blows with. It's not you against the world. It's not you against your audience. It's not you against your friends or your family. It's you versus yourself—your old self—and there is a definite winner and a definite loser. Luckily, you have the greatest advantage in this fight: you choose who wins and who loses.

Whenever life presents an opportunity for you to step closer to your goals and grow, you take it! No matter how afraid you are or how loud the old you screams "No!" draw your sword, cut the old you down, and yell your war-cry, "Yes!"

Choose to approach life this way from now on. Pledge to pick up your sword and prepare to fight each and every day because we've got work to do. Read on.

—Cody's Note—

I just finished watching the movie *Gladiator* **before writing this chapter and might have gotten carried away with the sword and shield analogy. You are welcome.**

CHAPTER 6

DEALING WITH THE PAST

After that fateful day talking with Jessica, I changed my tactics from trying to improve my performance to trying to control my fears. I read books like *Awaken The Giant Within* by Tony Robbins and *Failing Forward* by John C. Maxwell. Two books I highly recommend.

I began to realize through those books, and others like them, that my performance was an outcome of my ability to face my fear and control my response. My prior poor performances were a symptom of my reaction to fear. Trying to improve my performance in front of a crowd without addressing my fears was like going to battle without a single weapon.

I needed to attack the source: my fears were made even stronger by focusing on past mistakes.

Through reading, it became painfully clear that I was the one who chose to see the past as a bad thing. I chose to see those mistakes as open wounds that would never heal. I had a choice to either let my past public speaking experiences hurt me and limit me, or recognize them as lessons.

6th grade Cody had a lot to say, but I only ever heard the bad things. I never thought to see the good side of that experience. I didn't believe anything good could have possibly come from failing in front of Ms. Dory's class. I never saw it because I didn't know to look for the positive side from that experience.

Before, I would ask myself, "Why am I so bad at this?"

My younger self would answer, "Because I've always been bad at this."

Tony Robbins taught me in his book to ask better questions to get better answers.

I started asking, "What could I learn from that experience in middle school?"

"I . . . I could have actually practiced giving my presentation."

I asked, "What else?"

"I could have worked on it earlier instead of the night before."

I asked, "What could I have done to truly face my fears in that moment?"

"I could have raised my hand to speak first instead of avoiding it by waiting until my name was called."

Soon that experience didn't appear so bad. It actually felt empowering to see it in a new light: as a mistake that could serve me rather than hinder me.

I started questioning all my previous experiences. It became clear just how much I had hurt myself.

Now it's your turn. Since you're reading this, I'm sure you can think of a time when you didn't do so hot in front of a crowd. Take some time to think back over that experience. It might be uncomfortable thinking back, but trust me with this one.

Visualize going through the experience again, and then afterwards ask yourself, "What can I learn from that experience?" I recommend writing down the lessons. You'd be surprised how quickly this can change your perspective of those past experiences.

Those memories might have been a harsh reminder to avoid public speaking experiences, but no more. Today let those memories serve you towards better future experiences.

After you go through and view those past mistakes with new eyes, thank yourself. You just did yourself a huge favor, even if it was painful.

With our past now supporting us, it's time to address the oversized elephant in the room: our fear.

CHAPTER 7

WHAT IS FEAR?

Let's start by describing the feeling of fear for what it really is: a bodily response to a perceived threat or consequence— whether real or not.

In fact, we don't even have to identify the specific fear for our body to react. We just perceive a threat, and our body reacts.

There are different levels in response to fear. Anywhere from butterflies in your stomach to a full-blown anxiety attack. Two people might step out onto the same stage, facing the same audience, with the same message, with the same level of knowledge of that message, but the two could respond completely differently.

One speaker might talk confidently, connect with the audience, and appear quite comfortable. The other speaker, however, might be stricken with fear, mutter and stumble through their speech, and appear very uncomfortable on stage.

Did the threat change? Nope! The threat of possible failure, of the audience not reacting, was constant for both speakers. The difference was in their individual perception of the threat.

The confident speaker most likely focused on delivering a message that would benefit his audience. He walked out on that stage, appreciative of his audience coming to hear him speak, and focused on his opportunity to inspire, persuade, or entertain the crowd. To him, speaking is an honor, and he looked forward to the moment he would speak his first word to his audience.

The other speaker did not approach the opportunity the same way. He did not really see it as an opportunity but more as a threat to his level of comfort and peace of mind. Every passing moment before he actually had to speak, the lump in his throat grew, making it impossible to swallow. Fearing every mistake he might make in front of his audience, he tried not to think about it. But the more he tried not to, the more he anticipated potential blunders, obsessing over it.

Every negative thought just kept adding to his already growing nerves and his reaction to his fears. By the time he was actually on stage, his perception became his reality as he started making the mistakes and blunders he couldn't stop thinking about.

The real lesson here is we chose how to perceive and react to the threat.

This is like the White Bear Phenomenon. The idea is simple. Picture a white bear in your head for five seconds. Now, for the next 60 seconds, DO NOT think about the white bear. Ready? Go!

60 seconds later

Okay, how did you do? Did you successfully not think about the white bear during the 60 seconds? If you are like most people, you probably had a hard time not thinking about the bear.

The more effort you put into not thinking about the white bear, the more you actually end up thinking about the white bear, getting to the point of obsessing about the bear.

Thus, focusing on the mistakes you don't want to make on stage makes it more likely you will mess up. So instead focus on being a courageous speaker who's excited and looking forward to speak and guess what might just happen ☺.

While you can choose not to focus on your fear, you should know your fears never go away. So don't think that if you don't focus on them, they will magically go away. The truth is . . .

CHAPTER 8

FEARS NEVER GO AWAY

John Maxwell taught that our fears never truly go away. They are with us forever in a never-ending dance between us and what we fear most. That was discouraging to hear. I wanted a magic pill that would wipe my fears clean leaving nothing behind.

That magic pill doesn't exist. However, I can choose who takes the lead: fear or myself. There is never a choice to not dance with fear. That is unavoidable. You, however, get to decide who gains control. Let that sink in. No one else but you has everything you need to control your fear. It is a tango between you and your coward self.

Clearly, I had let my fears take the lead, and I was simply following their direction without question. But unfortunately, accepting that I had a choice did not make it easy to try to take the lead. I had been a follower for so long that taking the lead felt very uncomfortable.

Just like in all areas of life, you're going to make mistakes in taking charge. Don't expect to not step on your own toes the first go around. You may attempt and fail, falling back into letting your old self take the lead. Don't let that discourage you. Your power to choose is yours to keep forever. Even if you are failing consistently, one of your ultimate goals here is to start seeing failure in a whole new light. Maybe you'll even start to see failing as a positive experience.

CHAPTER 9

FAILING IS A BLESSING

So far we've worked hard to drive home the idea (or rather the fact) that we have a choice to make with how we view the world around us and what words we choose to use. We have a choice as to whether or not we will let fear call the shots. We get to choose and with that choice comes taking responsibility for our lives.

You get to choose how you see your failures. You can choose to see failure as something to avoid at all costs, to regret, to be embarrassed about—or—you can choose to see it as a blessing, though that might be contrary to popular belief.

All throughout school, we are taught that failure is bad. The inability to test well in school could result in failing the grade altogether, requiring one to repeat that grade while all their friends and previous classmates move on to the next grade. Getting an "F" on a report card for failing several assignments and/or tests can cause one to feel inferior.

This problem can then escalate to future failing grades, leading to one not receiving scholarships and/or being rejected by several colleges, resulting in living a mediocre life working at a gas station, struggling with money, and constantly wishing and dreaming for better things.

This, of course, is an extreme exaggeration. Obviously good grades or bad grades do not control our fate, our success, or our happiness after graduation.

Rather than this ingrained idea that failure is a terrible thing, I want us to view failure from a different lens. Let's look at it as a part of life. A part of simply being alive. Not something to avoid but to expect. Life happens. Failure happens. To each and every one of us.

Can you think of one person who has never failed at something? Someone who is perfect and gets everything right the first time? If you have, I would love to meet your imaginary friend! For now, I'm going to believe you have not. Everyone fails. Once you start to accept failure as a normal part of life, failing doesn't quite have the sting it once had.

Humans fail from the moment they are born. Just watch any infant learn to hold their head up right. At first it's a real struggle to balance that proportionally massive head on that spaghetti thin neck. Slowly but surely, they will gain more control and will no longer need assistance. Soon they can hold themselves upright while on their stomachs which becomes the prerequisite for crawling. A few more months, they master standing after much trial and error. Finally, they take that first step succeeded by yet another step reinforced by praise and excitement from two very proud parents.

The amount of "failing" leading up to that first step is staggering. Not even worth counting due to the sheer frequency of making mistake after mistake. Over and over that infant would try, fail, and try again gaining valuable experience with each attempt. Failure is not a means to an end but really a means to success. Failure from the beginning of all humans' lives is simply a way of life, and just a possible result of an attempt. That's it!

Adults are reluctant to try again after one failed attempt. Infants don't even question the result. They almost immediately try again without hesitation. I challenge you to see failure the same way—a step toward whatever your goal may be.

Start seeing failure as a blessing. A blessing that brings you closer to what you want. When viewed this way, failures take on a positive connotation. You're not likely to try and avoid a blessing. Why would you? Once you change your belief of failure from negative to positive, failure becomes one less reason to not try something and one less reason to be afraid. That's one less reason why you shouldn't be punching your fears IN. THE. FACE.

You: If failing should be a positive thing, then why am I so afraid?

Now that's a great question and the next chapter is going to answer that very question. Let's do this!

CHAPTER 10

WHY ARE YOU AFRAID?

Have you ever been around a 4-or 5-year-old kid who has discovered that magical, one-word question to help quench their unquenchable curiosity: "why?" This one word alone has the power to drive parents and loved ones alike absolutely insane if used correctly. Young children use that one question to help them understand and make sense of the world around them. We will use that very same question to help make sense of our fears.

This exercise can be done with anything you're afraid of. But for the purpose of this book, I want you to focus on your fear of public speaking.

Ask yourself, why you are afraid, and then once you write down the answer, ask why again.

This can be done with a partner asking you why after every answer or you can do it by yourself. I have my responses to the questions to give you an example.

Why am I afraid of public speaking?

- I'm afraid of looking stupid in front of a crowd and feeling judged.

Cool, why?

- Because looking stupid makes me feel uncomfortable

Cool, why?

- Because feeling smart or at least appearing smart gives me a sense of worth

Cool, why?

- Because having a sense of worth means to me that I have value and add value to others

Cool, why?

- Because without a sense of value, I feel worthless

Cool, why?

- If people think I'm worthless, no one will like me.

Cool, why?

- If no one likes me, then I might end up alone.

Ultimately, I'm afraid public speaking would reveal that I'm not as cool or important as I think I am. As if my sense of importance or worth was directly correlated to people liking me, and if people like me, then I have a good chance of having friends and not being alone. Being on stage might reveal and expose all my flaws, and then no one would want to be around someone so imperfect.

Sounds shallow, but that is something I desire: having value and thus being desired and accepted by others.

Once I recognized that, I actually felt better, to be honest. My fear was completely irrational, as most fears are. I'm not really afraid of speaking in public, I'm afraid of people realizing I'm not perfect. Everyone is flawed; no one is perfect, and we accept that of others, but sometimes we struggle to accept that of ourselves. My friends and family already know I'm not perfect, but accept me anyway.

Really take some time to get to the heart of your fears. It's important to do this before moving on to the next step where we walk through an exercise envisioning our worst fears coming to life.

WHAT IF IT REALLY HAPPENS?

Now that we've discovered what our greatest fears are, we are going to imagine what would happen if our greatest fears morphed their way into reality. The most important thing you can do is have fun with this.

I want you to write out the worst thing that could happen if your greatest fears came to life. I provided an example from my life below.

Now what if I actually completely failed on stage (which I've already done several times before), but this time my failure was not something I nor my reputation could recover from. The result? All my friends decide from that point onward they never want to see me again, my family disowns me, and Uncle Sam decides to discharge me from the Air Force because there is no chance the military would want to associate the armed forces with a failure such as myself.

To top it off, all the major news channels around the world run a news bit on my catastrophic failure, globally destroying my reputation and self-worth complete with others shaming me on social media sites. I then receive what seems like an endless supply of death threats in the mail. Now that—that would be my worst fears coming to life.

The likelihood of that ever happening? Practically never which equals a 0.0000000002% chance of actually coming to life if I were to just do the rough math off the top of my head. I have better chances legally identifying myself as a shark than ever experiencing what I just described.

If I'm being honest, I actually had fun writing it down, and I recommend you do that same after going through the "why?" exercise getting to the root of your fears. There is a weird sense of liberation after getting it on paper, and the more ridiculous you can make your outcome the funner (not a word) it is.

Once you're done, share your worst fears coming to life with someone. It's almost guaranteed to result in sheer, joyful laughter for the both of you. Share it with a group if you dare ☺.

Laughing at your greatest fears turns them on their heads and helps you realize just how ridiculous they really are and how insane it is to let your fears stop you.

Do that exercise and get ready for the next part where we will write down what we would do if our greatest fears really happened. We're going to ask ourselves. . .

SO WHAT?

Once again, I encourage you to have fun with this. I definitely did, and so did my wife and my buddy, Robert, after I read it out loud to them. Below is my example of what I would do if my world came crashing down.

What would I seriously do if my worst fear became reality? First off, I would probably be homeless without a job to pay bills or friends or family to lean on for help. The first few nights would probably be awful trying to get restful sleep outside on a park bench somewhere.

On the bright side, I would have a lot more free time throughout my day to wander the city. I'd eventually get over my pride and search dumpsters for food, discovering a hoard of food thrown away by large-chain grocery stores because they simply reached their "sell by" date.

Food would no longer be an issue, and I believe I would share my haul of goods with my fellow homeless tribe members. I'd become a Robin Hood of sorts among the homeless. Finally, I'd grow out my beard, thus hiding my original identity as the global speaking failure.

Once I grew my confidence for taking care of myself and ridding myself of my attachment to money, I would roam the United States as a nomad finally quenching my never-ending thirst to travel and experience the world around me. I would take my time wherever I went truly taking in my surroundings rather than prior vacations with a set agenda rushing from place to place to get my "money's worth." My days would be full of actually living instead of living vicariously through work, emails, Facebook, and keeping up with the latest technology.

I would finally be able to live in the moment versus constantly worrying about the future or regretting what happened in the past. I wouldn't be addicted to constantly checking my phone for notifications or text messages. I would have genuine conversation with people, and I wouldn't care at all which way the economy was swinging. I would have no sense of the latest "news," which before just filled me with fear and depression.

Eventually, the world would forget about my blunder—as with all things. I would have an opportunity to rejoin society, but I believe I would rather continue on living as a nomad free of modern worries and obligation.

That doesn't seem so bad anymore. Going through that exercise put a smile on my face. It forced me to actually walk through my fears instead of filling my day with tasks to keep my mind off my biggest fears. What I thought was a 10 on a scale of worst possible outcomes quickly dwindled down well below a 3. Before I believed if I failed, my life would be over, but really my life would just take a different direction. I realized, even if that happened, I could dig myself out of that hole.

It changed my perspective, and I hope it helps change yours. Don't forget to share this exercise with someone. It's bound to get another laugh.

So far we've spent several chapters knee deep in our fears, understanding why they have prevented us from wanting to face them head on. In this next section of the book, we are going to get waist deep to talk about ways to drop kick our fears in the face. But first, I want you to know . . .

CHAPTER 11

NOT ALL FEARS
ARE CREATED EQUAL

In the section discussing how to become a courageous speaker, I will challenge you to speak in public once a week in order to learn how to face your fears.

You: Well if facing my fears is the end goal, then can I just simply face a fear of mine once a week and skip this public speaking thing altogether?

Theoretically you could, but that is not bound to work out that well because not all fears are created equal. For example, the fear of asking someone out on a date via text message versus asking someone out in person versus asking someone out in front of all of her friends and yours have different levels and flavors of fear.

Asking someone out on a date over a text message leaves you feeling secure regardless of the outcome because you don't have to get rejected in person, and the feedback you get is limited to text, which means you don't get feedback from facial expression or tone of voice. (We'll ignore how asking someone out over text is totally not a groovy thing to do.)

Asking someone out in person has greater consequences if their answer is "no" because of the amount of feedback we receive from the pause in their response, the look in their eyes, the tone of their voice, their emotional response, and so on.

Compare that to asking them out in front of other people, which raises the stakes thereby raising the sting from a rejection. Not only do you receive a feeling of rejection from the "rejecter" (you being the rejectee—yes, I just made up that word) but also from the response of those around you, which could exponentially make the rejection feel worse.

Given a choice, we would probably choose the level of fear by weighing out the risk of each situation, disregarding which environment might increase your odds of acceptance. Since we are more likely to avoid pain rather than chase pleasure, the text message option remains the "safest" choice.

We'll do the same thing every week when choosing which fear to face. The path of least resistance, the lowest level of fear, will almost always be the one we choose to tackle nine times out at ten. We'll lean toward gathering low-hanging fruit compared to slaying our greatest demons.

Public speaking is arguably one of the greatest demons we can slay because we are exposed and vulnerable. This makes public speaking one of the best choices to face your fears on a weekly basis. Even if it's not your greatest fear, it's bound to be high on your list; otherwise, you probably wouldn't be reading this book.

Facing your fears of public speaking on a weekly basis creates an incredible environment for you to land an uppercut while becoming a courageous speaker. Once conquered, lesser fears seem less significant and easier to face. Fears on par with public speaking don't seem as insurmountable.

Once you conquer public speaking, other fears show their true colors as merely mental obstacles you can overcome because you already know how.

SECTION 3

—

HOW TO FACE ANY FEAR

CHAPTER 12

GIVE YOURSELF
PERMISSION TO SUCK

While not all fears are created equal, there are tools to help you face any fear. For the purposes of this book, I want you to apply these tools to public speaking. But once you have become a courageous speaker, remember you can apply these tools to help you defeat other fears holding you back.

For a long time, I was really hard on myself for making mistakes while speaking. I focused on the audience judging me but all along I was judging myself. You might have experienced the same. I'm here to tell you to cut yourself some slack! To properly karate chop our fears, we are going to focus on two things in this chapter:

1) Your goal is not perfection, your goal is to get in front of people and speak—often.

2) You are going to make mistakes—look forward to them. They will either be your best friend or your worst enemy.

Go ahead and say the following out loud to yourself.

"From this moment on I, [STATE YOUR NAME], give myself permission to suck."

There, I'm glad we got that out of the way. That statement helps lower the expectations that we put on ourselves. It doesn't mean we don't try or don't care. It's actually the opposite but with a twist.

You should want to try hard, do well, and care enough about speaking that you strive for a high standard. However, you also need to understand the importance of leaving room for making mistakes.

Giving yourself permission to suck also helps guide you away from the mindset that mistakes will lead to failure. That viewpoint taken to extreme levels can prevent you from even trying altogether.

We want to move away from that initial response to avoid mistakes, and instead, learn to embrace mistakes. This helps us focus on mistakes for what they truly are rather than perceiving them as bad things that we must prevent at all costs.

Once that's clear to you, your viewpoint of the world will start to change. The old you would see an opportunity and ask:

"Is there a chance I could fail?"

That is the wrong question to ask. Of course there is a chance you could fail. That question will stand between your old self and your new self. That question keeps you exactly where you're standing, with no chance of moving forward.

Make your decisions based on a better question:

"Is there a chance for me to grow, expand my comfort zone, face my fears, and/or learn lessons I can use to become a better version of myself?"

That type of question sets you up for success. Answering that question already moves you closer in the direction of your public speaking goals because you will almost always answer with "Yes!" There are hardly any speaking opportunities where you won't expand your comfort zone, face your fears of speaking, and/or learn a lesson through that experience! If you do answer "no," then that opportunity is not for you.

Choosing to ask and answer the second question doesn't leave room for your old self to share his opinion. Since you have given yourself permission to suck, the first question is obsolete. You don't care if you suck or not. You care if you learn, grow, and/or face your fears.

Sucking or not sucking is not important at this stage. What's important is getting in front of people as much as possible regardless of the outcome.

Which sounds better:

"I spoke in public, failed, and made a lot of mistakes."

Or

"I went out there, tried, and learned a lot of lessons."

The literal words you use have serious power on your attitude and how you approach life. You have a choice to choose the words you will use to describe your experiences, your future opportunities, and your overall outlook on life.

For example the old you might say,

"I wasn't born for public speaking."

"I have never been good at speaking, so I never will."

"I have always been too afraid to speak in front of crowds."

"It does not matter how much I try I will never get better."

This type of self-talk leaves no room for other possibilities. These are lies we tell ourselves, and from what I learned from Tony Robbins, these lies fall into the category of "safe problems."

Everyone has a safe problem. We use it as a crutch or excuse as to why we can or can't do something, whatever that might be. If I believe that I wasn't born to speak in public, that's my excuse to justify not speaking in public, avoiding opportunities to speak, or not trying my hardest when I'm obligated to speak. It's lazy and cowardly. I would know since I used to tell myself the same things. I told myself those statements so many times I truly believed the lies. I drank my own Kool-Aid so to speak.

It was easier to believe I had an excuse than to put in more effort or accept what I didn't want to believe. I didn't want to admit I was a coward. It hurt to admit it. It hurt badly. But eventually, I realized there was no one else to blame but me.

I remember when I finally whispered to myself, "I'm truly just a coward" and started to cry. That was a low point for me, but it was the moment of weakness I needed to start finding my greatness, stop making excuses for myself, and start using different words that built me up instead of holding me back.

I was finally willing to accept that I got myself into this mess and I would have to get myself out. In order to accept the mistakes I would make, I had to give myself permission to suck.

Now that you have given yourself permission to suck, you are ready to start slaying this demon. In order to slay this demon, and really any fear, you will need discipline, courage, confidence, principles to follow, and the commitment to take action. So let's talk about how we cultivate those.

CHAPTER 13

DISCIPLINE IS A PUSH

Previously, we dove into what holds us back. Now, we are ready to enter the land of tools, tricks, and concepts that will help us speak in public like the courageous speaker we know we can be. The first concept is my good friend, discipline.

Discipline is the push to do what you know you need to do, even though it might make you feel uncomfortable. It's that faint voice in your head that's trying to get through your thick skull. We've all heard it. Sitting on the couch halfway through a family size bag of cool ranch Doritos while binge watching *The Office*, you catch a glimpse of your running shoes by the door. Your mind drifts back to three months ago when you committed to run three times a week.

You hear a voice in your head say, "I really should go for a run." You know you need to, but you just don't feel motivated to run. Here is the truth about motivation: it's a fickle thing. Motivation is not always there when you really need it. To be honest, it only seems to show up when you are actively doing something you want to do. Right now you are motivated to stay on the couch. You start

65

to have a little pity party for dropping the ball. Then you hear a different voice.

"Work has been tough lately, and I just haven't had the energy to run."

"Today is the first day in weeks I've had time to myself."

"It's chilly outside, and it might rain."

"I might injure myself."

"I can always run tomorrow."

"I worked hard this week and deserve a break, one more day won't hurt me."

Your old self really has a foot in the door now, leading you to feel comfortable pushing off the run for another day. Any reason to stay on the couch and scarf down the rest of those Doritos gets red-carpet treatment into the land of sound reason.

However, you know eventually you will have to recognize these are simply masked excuses. You shovel another mouthful of chips to distract yourself from going down that train of thought. . . .

But clear as day, you hear "You made a promise!"

"Remember how you felt three months ago when the elevator broke in the office building at work, and you had to use the stairs to go up two flights of stairs to your floor?"

Thinking back again, you remember struggling to make it up to your floor, huffing and puffing. You made a pit stop in the bathroom, locked yourself in a stall, and started pulling at the collar of your shirt to cool off as you started to sweat. It was embarrassing.

After an extended stay in the stall, you stepped out just to look at yourself in the mirror. You felt angry for letting things go as far as they have. You promised yourself to run three times a week because you never wanted to feel that way again.

The memory almost makes you feel worse. Instead of being encouraged/motivated, it actually makes you want to just forget the whole thing ever happened.

"At least try. Put your shoes on and step outside. If afterwards you still don't want to run, you can come back inside. Deal?"

You figured the simple act of putting on shoes and stepping outside is not a far stretch outside your level of comfort. You brush off the Dorito crumbs from your shirt and make your way to the door. Putting on your shoes makes it crystal clear that they are practically brand new. You've hardly worn them at all since buying them the same day the elevator broke three months ago.

Stepping outside, you immediately feel the chilly wind. Looking around the neighborhood, the cold air wakes you up from the drowsiness caused by hours of snacking and sitting on the couch.

At that moment, you decide you might as well go for a walk since you're already outside. A walk seems harmless enough. At least you'll get a little bit of exercise today. A short walk becomes a long walk, and before you realize it, you've picked up your pace. Walking turns into running, without even much of a thought.

You're sweating profusely. Your joints ache. Your lungs are on fire. Ten minutes of running, and you find yourself wheezing. You stop to catch your breath, and you notice the cold wind cutting your throat as you breathe. The formation of a blister from your new shoes is evident.

You feel awful—but—you can't believe what came from the simple act of putting on your shoes and stepping outside. Smiling, you realize just 20 minutes ago you were accepting defeat. Finally, you thought to yourself, *I can do this!*

All you needed was the discipline to put on your shoes and step outside. Everything else fell into place. After you're already outside with your shoes on, it only takes a little discipline to simply start walking. After that, it only takes a little more discipline to turn walking into running.

However, it takes a lot of discipline to go from sitting on the couch to full on running when you really don't want to. You would need the discipline to go from a place of comfort (sitting on the couch) to a place of discomfort (running, sweating, and exhaustion). In comparison, the discipline to simply put on your shoes is insignificant in comparison. Once that's done, you just need a small morsel of discipline to step outside. Next, let the domino effect continue.

Instead of having the discipline to run three times a week, you just need the discipline to put on your running shoes three days a week. I'm sure you would have no problem convincing yourself to do something so simple.

Putting on your running shoes three days a week soon becomes five days a week. Running for a few minutes becomes a few miles. Those new shoes aren't so new anymore.

After some time, what originally caused you to feel out of breath during that first run is hardly a warmup for you now. Afterwards you feel invigorated and missing a run actually makes you feel noticeably less energetic.

Running hills, in snow, in rain or in the heat of summer are tough mentally and physically, but you have enough endurance built up to carry you through.

Of course you've experienced bumps and bruises and blisters along the way. Tripped a time or two. They might have slowed you down, but they certainly didn't stop you from putting on your shoes the next day.

Facing your fears of public speaking has a very similar approach. You will need the discipline to do the very next step. The discipline needed to speak in front of a crowd on a regular basis seems like a daunting amount, especially if your approach thus far was to stay far away from any chance of having to speak.

However, it doesn't take a lot of discipline to read an affirmation in the morning to help you feel positively about seeking out public-speaking opportunities (we'll talk more about affirmations later in the book). Just like it doesn't take much discipline to put on your running shoes, it doesn't take much discipline to seek public-speaking opportunities. Just like walking didn't take much effort once you were already outside with your shoes on, it only takes a little more discipline to say "Yes" to public-speaking opportunities.

Walking can be compared to showing up to a local public-speaking club like Toastmasters (we'll talk more about Toastmasters later in the book). Since you're already there, you might build up the nerve to do a two minute speech in front of everyone. Now your walk turned into a run, and you didn't even plan for it.

CHAPTER 14

COURAGE IS THE PULL

After implementing the steps in this book, your first speech still may not go well. It could very well be awful, but once it's over, you will think to yourself, *I can do this!*

Discipline is the push and courage is the pull. The two work together to push and pull you toward your better self when you are afraid. Motivation only shows up after you start seeing results, not before. That's why you cannot depend on being motivated to get you through your fears. You need discipline to take the first step and courage to make the next step easier.

Courage is built through taking action to face our fears. Just like you may not have a lot of muscle the first time you start working out, you don't necessarily start off with courage. Over time, your muscles start to grow. Courage is a muscle.

In the beginning, lifting a certain amount of weight might seem difficult. However, building muscle over time makes that same amount of weight easier to lift and move. With courage, what might have seemed terrifying at first becomes less scary over time.

If you consistently work at building courage, those terrifying speaking opportunities will be a piece of cake.

There is one catch. Stop running and your endurance will seemingly cease to exist. Stop using your muscles, and your strength will take a hike. Stop using your courage to speak, and it will fade away. Courage is either lost, maintained, or gained. It is not a resource that remains at a constant supply without effort on your behalf.

CHAPTER 15

COURAGE CROSS TRAINING

The steps in this book will help you gain and maintain a healthy dose of courage to truly become a courageous speaker. This courage will certainly carry over to other aspects of your life. Consider building courage while speaking in front of a crowd as cross training for your other goals that you are afraid to pursue.

Usually our fear of trying anything (from my experience) stems from two basic fears:

- Fear of rejection

- Fear of failure

These two fears hit me like a ton of bricks when I first thought about writing this book. Boy did my coward self have a heyday as the following thoughts raced through my brain:

1. Who would care what I have to say?

2. Don't I need to be an "expert" to even consider writing a book in this area?

3. I got C's in English in school.

4. What if everyone hates my book?

5. What if I can't think of enough to even write about?

6. Am I too young for people to take me seriously?

7. What if I don't even finish and waste a bunch of time and effort for nothing?

I was in a bad state of mind. I could only picture my book on Amazon with several 1 star reviews with people bashing my book, sending my reputation as a speaker down the toilet. I limited my chances of success because I was afraid my book would be a complete failure and people would say it wasn't even worth reading.

My fears got the best of me, which is ironic considering I wanted to write a book about overcoming fears of public speaking. But there I was drenched in my fears of writing and publishing a book.

That went on for weeks as I really considered giving up on the idea all together. I didn't snap out of that funk until I asked myself out of frustration,

"Why do I even want to write this stupid book??"

I remember sitting in my car stuck in typical Los Angeles grade traffic, gripping my steering wheel, and verbalizing that question. I sat on that question for a few minutes trying to really uncover why I wanted to write the book. My first thought was "because writing a book sounds cool." It did sound cool, but that was not a great reason to write a book.

I decided to calm down and ask a better question, "Who am I writing this for?" That was an easy question to answer. I wanted to write for anyone who is afraid of public speaking and who wanted to know how to conquer their fears. I wanted to help people determine when their old, coward-self was talking versus when their courageous-self had the floor. Ultimately, I wanted to help more people punch their fears in the face.

It wasn't until then that I finally realized I was letting my fears take control, just like back in high school at the beginning of my journey to become a great public speaker. I just had to stop and laugh because I knew what I needed to do to overcome my fears. I must have subconsciously assumed that since I was not getting ready to speak, the techniques I would need to get rid of this fear would be different.

That train of thought was completely wrong. All I needed to do was to have a small amount of discipline to take the first step. Then I would need just a small amount of discipline to take the next step. If I could do that on a consistent basis, I would eventually build enough courage to keep going even if I were afraid.

I've faced my fears before with public speaking, which for me was a bigger fear to conquer compared to writing a book. So clearly, unless I let myself get in the way, there was no reason I couldn't accomplish this goal. I was being my biggest critic before even writing a single word for this book. I'd already overcome bigger mountains. That perspective made my fears of writing seem so small in comparison.

Suddenly, I felt empowered again with all of my experience facing my fears behind me backing me up. Without that, I probably would have just simply given up before I even started. I've done that more times than I would like to count.

I imagine you might have done the same a time or ten. Just like me, you probably thought about doing something, but your coward self shot down that idea before it could even attempt to take flight. It was immediately deemed too risky due to a chance of failure and cast aside.

You might not have much experience consistently facing your fears to draw on when attempting something new. Without that foundation to stand on, your coward self doesn't have to try very hard to pull the rug out from under you.

Now imagine you have consistently faced one of your biggest fears, speaking in public, on a regular basis. Imagine your courageous self having a voice whenever you attempt to face your fears so now your coward self is not the only one speaking. It becomes a fight between the two. Since your coward self only has hypothetical situations of future failures that will most likely never come to pass, it has to fight harder. Your courageous self has all of your past experience to back him up. Facts are hard to deny. Ultimately, you will have to decide whom to choose. You get to decide whether your journey will be a stage fight or a stage fright. Let that empower you. Here, in the Stage Fight Club, there's really only one choice. Hint: it's in the title ☺.

CHAPTER 16

BUILDING CONFIDENCE

I chose the title of this chapter very carefully. I kept it short and cut away everything else that I considered non-essential. Two words—two words could almost summarize the entire purpose of this book. It's incredible what can be pulled from such a short phrase, and I would like you to read those two words out loud before diving into the meat of this section. Read them slowly. Slow enough that you start to picture in your head images of what those words bring to mind. Go ahead and do that now.

When I read them slowly, various images came to mind. Yours might be similar or completely different.

Build: I pictured a home starting from a plot of land being built before my very eyes. Day and night flashed by in rapid succession before the home was complete. That quickly morphed into a skyscraper surrounded by large cranes rising higher and higher as the building neared completion.

Confidence: I pictured a man in a business suit giving a quarterly report to a board of directors in a fortune 500 company. I pictured a young woman leading a community outreach event of 100+

volunteers helping the homeless. I pictured a mechanic elbow deep into the turbine engine of a jet locating and fixing the source of a major malfunction.

Each word will spark images, formed by pieces of our own life experiences and our perception of the world around us.

By thinking on these two words and the images they conjure, you bring meaning and life to the idea of building confidence.

So let's start with the word "build."

Build is a verb—the action part of the phrase, insinuating that something must be physically done to complete the phrase. We must take action. Action towards whatever we want to build confidence in. Here, in the Stage Fight Club, we want to build confidence in public speaking.

The image that comes to mind when thinking of the word "build" is more often than not something tangible like a home or roads or you name it.

But now let's look at confidence; it is intangible. You can't touch it, smell it, hear it, or see it. Confidence is not made of matter or energy. It is more an assurance of our ability to perform an action. Confidence is experienced through the results of having it or not having it.

You can't see it as it grows, but you can certainly feel it grow within you over time, but only if you nurture it. In the short term, you may not notice it. Over the long term, you and others will notice that confidence. It is a slow subconscious change; therefore, you can't determine the exact moment your confidence increased.

In a world filled with instant satisfaction, it's all too easy to give up on building anything that takes significant time and effort to notice results.

You will not necessarily notice any improvements right away. However, once you put in the time, the difference between your first speech and one you give after months of consistently building your confidence will be night and day.

However, since these changes are subtle, I have someone record every time I speak. Every few months I'll go back and re-watch my performances compared to my most recent one, and every time I'm surprised by how much I've improved. I highly recommend you do the same.

Building confidence is a personal endeavor. You must take action to build your confidence. No one else can do it for you. You cannot buy it. You cannot watch a video on confidence and build it. You cannot read books about building confidence and build it.

You must literally expend energy and effort into action to build it. Action takes effort and effort is work. In this case, building confidence in public speaking can take a lot of work. Work that might not show results until a significant amount of time has passed. I would argue the amount of time can be seriously shortened by following the steps in this book.

You have to take ownership of building your confidence. That journey is yours. The path is yours to take. The choice to build your confidence is yours to choose.

CHAPTER 17

FOUR INITIAL
PRINCIPLES AT PLAY

As you build your confidence, there are some basic principles that apply to all your fears. If you learn and implement these principles, you will be able to conquer them.

During the summer of 2014, nine months after I had researched ways to control my fears, I had my first opportunity to implement the principles I had learned and face my fears head on.

School was out, and I was stoked about our church's youth group mission trip to Arlington, Texas.

Our youth Pastor, Byron, decided he wanted the student leaders to give speeches on certain topics every night of the week in Texas. He went around the table pairing students to speak Monday through Friday.

"Josh and Nick are on Monday. Candice and Allison on Tuesday. . . ." By the time he got through Thursday, my name had not been called. I was relieved. At this point, the odds were in my favor as there were twelve other juniors and seniors left to choose from. He only needed two more students for Friday, so I figured I was home free.

". . . and Cody and Lynley will speak Friday on the butterfly effect and how it relates to a story in the Bible." My heart stopped, and I felt my gut explode. I must have made a face because Byron spoke to me after the meeting was over.

He said if I needed help, he had a story I could incorporate in my speech. I think I flat out told him that I did. He gave me a story that I could tell about how a man inspired his father, Ray, to become a pastor, suggesting I reveal at the end that the story was about his father, who in turn inspired him to become a pastor as well.

Even with this head start, I was afraid to speak. I even considered not going at all on the mission trip, giving the money away to a family who needed it.

Trust me, this was a big deal. I had spent the last four months selling Avon bug spray with my brothers outside of Walmart trying to save money to go on the trip. If speaking was my #1 fear, selling something to strangers was definitely a close 2nd.

But in the end, I decided to go on the trip.

Everything I had learned so far about facing my fears discouraged running away and avoiding them. I'd already committed to overcoming my fear of public speaking and replacing it with courage.

I knew it wasn't going to be easy, but I also knew I was sick and tired of being a coward. This had affected too much of my life already and speaking in front of a crowd of 100+ students on this mission trip was a huge step in the right direction.

I believed in four principles at this point:

1. Running away from my fears actually makes things worse.

2. The only mistake is not trying.

3. It is okay to be nervous.

4. Give yourself permission to suck.

But just because you believe something doesn't mean you won't be afraid, screw up, or fail when putting what you believe into practice.

I closely held onto those principles during my time on the mission trip.

I gave myself leeway to make mistakes while facing my fears, knowing I could then learn from them, making me a better speaker.

Whenever I would start to panic during our trip out to Texas, which was usually during the evening when the other student pairs were giving their speeches, I would pull out a note card with those four statements and read them. I would focus on them so I could start to settle back down. While reading the cards did not take my fears away, it did stop my fears and anxiety from getting out of control.

The whole week I practiced my speech more than I've ever practiced before. Whenever I had some free time, I would practice alone under a stairwell or anywhere I could find some privacy. I would rehearse and revise until I finally had a finished product.

I worked hard because I wanted this time to be different. I can truthfully say it certainly felt different, but I was still extremely nervous. Nervous enough that I made note cards with my main points just in case I forgot any of them because I was still holding on to the belief that I needed help, and I couldn't do it on my own.

On Friday, I went into the meeting hall an hour early to calm my nerves. I had rehearsed enough, but I needed to find something to do to keep my mind busy. I knew if I let my nerves run wild, it would only make things worse.

I looked around the room for something to do and noticed the 100+ envelopes taped to every wall in the room. Each envelope had someone's name on it from our group. They were there so we could leave encouraging notes to each other throughout the week.

I had already written a few but only to close friends. That seemed like the perfect way to keep my mind busy. I decided to write everyone an encouraging note within the hour I had left.

Feverishly, I started writing everyone a note. It came down to the wire, but I managed to write about 120 notes before everyone started making their way into the room. I held those encouraging notes in my hand and prayed over them, hoping they would make the recipient's day brighter.

After the prayer I felt much better. I was still very nervous but for once before giving a speech, I was surprisingly calm.

I got up from where I was sitting and made my way around the room, putting the notes into each of the envelopes. When I got to the last envelope, I actually had a few notes left over. I just assumed I wrote too many and thought nothing of it.

Byron started going through the laundry list of things we needed to hear before Lynley and I spoke. I could hardly pay attention to what Byron was saying because I was doing everything I could to keep my nerves in check.

I mainly just focused on my four points, especially the third point: it's okay to be nervous. My heart raced like I was about to go to war after receiving news from my commanding officer that the expected survival rate for our mission was less than 8%. I reminded myself that being nervous was simply a signal from my body that I felt this was important.

So I took the time to actually think about why I was going to give this speech. I had spent so much time and energy focusing on what I was going to do and say that I never took a second to think about why. I asked myself why, and my brain answered, "Because Byron told me to." That was not a good answer.

That answer pointed a finger at Byron as if he was forcing me to speak, and he was the one to blame. That answer would just put up another mental barrier I would have to get through, and I already had several walls to bust through as it was.

That answer came from the old me, so I asked a question only the new me could answer: "Why is this important?" My brain responded, "Because someone in this crowd could really use what you have to say." That answer changed my perspective. Instead of seeing it from my perspective, I was seeing it through the eyes of someone in the audience who could actually benefit from what I had to say.

That changed everything. That answer gave my message an actual purpose. A reason why. I actually smiled thinking this could help someone.

"Now I'd like to call up our student speakers, Cody and Lynley, to the front to give tonight's message," Byron said, and . . . my smile went away.

Lynley went first.

I truly don't remember many details about her speech because in the middle of her speaking, I felt the nerves get the better of me, so I decided to look over the key points I had written on notecards.

I reached into my pocket and pulled them out. To my surprise, I pulled out encouraging notes instead. I checked the rest of my pockets and found nothing. Then it dawned on me. I had extra notes left which meant I accidentally mixed up my key points with the encouraging notes earlier. A few people actually received my key points rather than encouragement.

The mystery was solved, but that realization did not help calm me down—it actually made me feel worse. There was nothing I could do at that point. I assumed without those notecards, my speech was dead on arrival. All that hard work for nothing.

I looked down at the encouraging note I wrote for someone else. It read:

Hey, I just wanted to tell you that you're doing a great job. You can't even imagine the great things that will come out of your hard work.

Maybe it was fate that I would write words of encouragement to myself. Those words were exactly what I needed. They grounded me. Brought me back to my center, and reminded me of why this was important.

I took a deep breath and heard, "and that's all I have to say. Thank you." Lynley just finished and everyone turned their attention toward me. My turn had come, and I began by asking everyone to give Lynley a round of applause.

Or that's what I meant to say. What I actually said was, "Let's giver a gate round of menopause."

The audience was deadpan silent. They looked at me like I had just spoken a different language, and in retrospect, I practically had.

Thank goodness I already gave myself permission to suck because I was off to a great start.

All I could think to do was start clapping. Luckily everyone gradually followed suit, probably to help cut through the awkward silence I just created, and with that, I started my speech. I took a deep breath and told the story of Ray.

In the middle of telling the story, I realized I had everyone's genuine attention. They were glued to every word I said. This had never happened before. The students and even adults were focused and leaning into what I had to say.

"What you don't know is that Ray's last name was Ray Malone, and his son's full name is Byron "Lee" Malone, our own youth pastor, and the reason we are all here today."

I just spilled the beans, and I could see it click in everyone's eyes as if I had just let them in on my little secret. I took advantage of the moment and took a second chance requesting a round of applause, but this time for Byron, our youth pastor.

Everyone responded with a heartfelt applause, and in that moment, I realized I didn't need my notes. I never did. It was actually a blessing to lose them. They were the shield I was holding onto. Something I could hide behind.

I felt alive, and for once I was glad my speech wasn't over. I still needed to tell the Bible story. I was on an autopilot now. Words were flowing out of me like I was born to speak.

I got into the story, acting out parts of it.

I was on fire. The old me was nowhere to be found, and the new me took a foothold. I didn't even stop at the end of my planned speech. I improvised and kept going.

The student body started clapping so loud it shocked me. I was so stunned by the response I almost started to cry. This has never happened before. I had never felt this way before after speaking. It filled my body with energy and thrilled me to new heights.

I gave the floor back over to Byron, and he ended the night with prayer just before it was time to send us off back to the hotel before lights out.

As I made my way through the room, I received words of encouragement and praise, more high fives than I've ever received before, hugs from people I hardly knew, and someone said to me, "I had no idea you could speak like that." All I could say back was, "I didn't either."

CHAPTER 18

ADDING MORE PRINCIPLES

That night after giving my speech, I was on cloud nine. It was like someone let an innocent man out of his mental prison. A prison I created and sentenced myself to. After all, I was my own jury and judge.

I felt too wired to sleep. As my mind started to wonder about why this time went so well and why all the other times went down the toilet, I realized I had approached the assignment completely different than all of my previous experiences. I practiced more than I had ever practiced before, practicing multiple times a day.

I also focused on those four principles:

1. Running away from my fears actually makes things worse.

2. The only mistake is not trying.

3. It is okay to be nervous.

4. Give yourself permission to suck.

Prior to this, I would simply focus on all my previous failures attempting to speak in public. But instead of concentrating on all of my past mistakes, I focused on those four statements. I zeroed in on each of them when I would get beyond nervous. Running away was no longer an option. I was going to try no matter what. I truly believed being nervous no longer indicated that I was not good enough. Rather, it meant I took the assignment seriously.

Lastly, I gave myself permission to suck. I made room to make mistakes and learn from them. I didn't hold myself to a ridiculously high standard.

Mulling over the events of that night, I recognized other principles. That night I asked myself why speaking was important? After realizing that there might be someone in the audience that could benefit from my message, I finally stopped focusing on myself, on my mistakes, or on my fears. Instead, I focused on whom my message might impact.

Focusing on benefiting my audience is a win-win. That helps me stop focusing on how nervous I am and reminds me there is a good chance someone in that crowd will learn from my message. I know I'm certainly not going to be able to please everyone by a long shot, but something I say or do during my speech will likely resonate with someone in the crowd. That was great feedback so I wrote down:

"It is not about me"

Continuing my thoughts about what made this time different, I realized I had told a story for the first time ever. Whenever my dad would tell a story, he would always give great details to draw you in. I love listening to him because his stories helped me understand what my dad was saying and relate to him.

That is exactly what happened during my speech. Had I just described the butterfly effect I would not have held the audience's attention. However, the story had aspects and details everyone could relate to. Those aspects connected my audience to my message on a personal level.

I had never told a story in my speeches before and didn't realize how powerful they are. As a bonus, I realized it is easier to tell a story on stage than to try and memorize an entire speech. This felt important so I wrote down the following:

"Tell a story"

And the last advice I could pull from that night was this:

"Know your audience is human"

The first half of that phrase has been tossed around since who knows when: "Know your audience." This means to know your audience well enough to understand what your audience would respond to best.

I took a different approach and extended the phrase to know your audience *is human*. You might ask why I would make that distinction. Sometimes we can forget that our audience is made up of humans. Humans with their own fears, flaws, and insecurities. There is a good chance 90% of your audience is also afraid to speak in public just like you. They aren't a panel of judges ready to throw old food at you and boo you off the stage the moment they smell weakness.

It's actually interesting to hear that your flaws actually help you connect with your audience. No one is perfect, and there isn't much benefit to appearing perfect. Just imagine being in the audience listening to someone brag about themselves, their amazing accomplishments, and how incredible their life is. How likely are you to relate and connect with someone like that? Compare that to a speaker who might be a little nervous and stumble a bit, but they talk about some struggles they've gone through in life, mistakes they've made, and how they overcame those obstacles. Now that would be someone I could connect with. I'm certainly not the greatest of speakers; I've struggled and made plenty of mistakes, so I can look up to someone who overcame obstacles even with their imperfect record.

Knowing my audience is human really struck me the next morning. I was still feeling great from the night before, and my pride wanted someone to tell me how great I was the night before. That never happened.

No one even mentioned my speech as if everyone just forgot all about it. That hurt a little bit, but it started to feel reassuring. If I had completely bombed last night, everyone still would have reacted the same the next morning. Whether I did great or terrible, they would have gone about their lives regardless. They probably forgot all about it five minutes after I was done speaking to be honest. Humans forget, which means the only person who truly remembers my mistakes is me. No one else really cares.

This meant there wasn't a single person from Ms. Dory's 6th grade class who remembered my horrible speech.

With that I added three more principles, giving me seven, to help me become a courageous speaker.

1. Running away from my fears actually makes things worse.

2. The only mistake is not trying.

3. It is okay to be nervous.

4. Give yourself permission to suck.

5. It is not about you

6. Tell a story

7. Know your audience is human

All of these principles helped me tremendously in my battle against my fears of public speaking. I hope they help you just as much if not more. Fortunately, this story doesn't end here. At this point, I had won the battle, but I wouldn't find out what it took to win the war until I went to Honduras.

CHAPTER 19

SHAPE YOUR LIFE BY TAKING ACTION OFTEN

In college after my Sophomore year, I took a week-long mission trip to Honduras. Prior to going, I did what I thought was the best way to learn Spanish. I spent three months over the summer learning vocabulary, using apps, and speaking broken Spanish to my wife whenever I thought about it.

I thought I was prepared for the trip, but it only took three minutes into speaking with a woman on the plane to realize I was nowhere close to speaking and understanding the language well.

I successfully accomplished confusing the two of us, and realized the only thing I could do was order off the menu at Taco Bell. Need a Quesadilla? I'm your guy.

During those three months, I felt like I was making significant headway. But my knowledge was hardly attached to any actual worldly experience using, listening to, and interpreting Spanish. All that time on my phone apps and running through flashcards of vocabulary was all bunk.

I was a little more than discouraged getting off the plane, knowing my efforts have been less than useful, but having a pity party was not going to do me any good either.

Most of the members of my team spoke fluent Spanish, so whenever possible, I would speak to them in Spanish. I would also dive into a conversation with the locals to supercharge my learning even though I was scared to look like an idiot. Most of the time, I would just get weird looks like I was a babbling idiot, which was probably accurate given the circumstances.

Three days in my Spanish improved significantly to the point I could gradually stop thinking in English and waste less time interpreting in my head. By the end of the week, I could carry on a conversation with a local well outside the typical "Hello, friend. My name is Cody. How are you?"

I could go to the marketplace and bargain prices for watermelons and other goods. Don't get me wrong I had a lot more to learn after only one week, but the difference between the Cody who flew into Honduras and the Cody who flew out of Honduras was staggering.

My success came from practicing it every day. Skipping even a day may have caused me to forget what I had learned the day before. Eight weeks after leaving Honduras, I had lost most, if not all, of my ability to speak Spanish. I was back to simply ordering food at Taco Bell for my non-Spanish speaking wife. My seven days of practicing was not enough to maintain the skill long term. If I had more days or years of experience, it would have taken longer to forget.

It makes sense that in order for knowledge and experience to be useful, they have to be maintained.

I'm not sure when I figured out I could apply the same thought process to public speaking, but at some point in the fall semester, I decided to experiment speaking as often as I could. I figured if I immersed myself in speaking on a weekly basis, I could see similar results as the ones from Honduras.

Through a lot of trial and error, I came up with a process that I've laid out in the following chapters of the book to show you how to punch your fears in the face on a regular basis and win the war.

We're going to talk about the importance of speaking once a week, how we can accomplish such a task, and best of all how we can have fun doing it. First things first, you'll need to know one thing to get started.

We, here in the Stage Fight Club (there is no rule about not talking about the Stage Fight Club), do not wish to slowly expand our comfort zone. We know life is too short to move slowly. No, we will chase after that future self like it's a hunt by building our lives around punching our fears you know where. In doing so, we'll put more and more distance between ourselves and our coward-selves daily. Yes, daily!

We know we cannot face our fears and stay within our own level of comfort. We cannot just simply read a book about public speaking to become a better public speaker. We cannot watch a video of a phenomenal speaker and expect to be better speakers by the time the video is over. In essence, we cannot grow without taking action. This book will not help you unless you put into action what you learn from reading it and actually start public speaking. Like I learned from my experience in Honduras, we have to take action often to maintain that ability. So let's dive in and start becoming a courageous speaker!

SECTION 4

—

HOW TO BECOME A
COURAGEOUS SPEAKER

CHAPTER 20

SPEAKING ONCE PER WEEK

Mistakes + Learning = Life Lessons
If you had the choice between overcoming your fears over a few months versus slowly over 10 years, what would you pick? As little time as possible, right? Who wouldn't? 10 years is a long time to battle fears and anxiety. That's the pull-the-Band-Aid-off-one-arm hair-at-a-time approach.

We, here in the Stage Fight Club, are hard core and don't even use Band-Aids, but if we did, we'd rip them off like greased lightning.

This clicked for me after Honduras. I simply determined I would speak in front of a crowd at least once a week to overcome my fears as fast as possible. More than once a week would accelerate my growth, but at least once a week was a good baseline.

And, of course, before you speak you have to practice, which gives you daily practice.

No boss wants to go to a quarterly meeting and have his employees wing it while they try briefing on how the last quarter went.

No congregation wants to go to church to hear a preacher wing his message on stage. That goes double for the choir.

No one pays to go to a comedy club to watch a comedian who didn't prepare their jokes, stories, or punchlines.

No one wants to listen to a keynote speaker who decided they would make it up as they go.

No one wants to hear the best man give a speech that was not prepared.

Practice goes hand-in-hand with overcoming our fears and anxieties as we keep moving forward to become our better selves. So not only will we practice speaking in public once a week, but we will practice daily for the event, maintaining and nurturing our skills even more.

I'll show you the many ways you can get in front of a crowd once a week later in this book. For now we'll stick with the *why* and we'll save the *how* for later.

Now when I say build your life around public speaking, I do not mean drop everything around you including work, family, health and sleep to become a great public speaker. That's a recipe for disaster. But we can all wrap our heads around speaking once a week.

You: Will that really be enough to overcome my fears?

Absolutely! That's 52 additional public speaking events you probably would not have intentionally sought-after. Do you think you would be a different person after 52 speeches in a year? I guarantee you will. There's no way not to be after that. However, it won't take you the whole year to notice a change. Four weeks is enough time to notice serious changes.

Now that you have committed to speak once a week, you will want to spend an hour each day preparing for your speech.

CHAPTER 21

IMPORTANCE OF COMMITTING AN HOUR A DAY

You: An hour a day? I hardly feel there's enough time in the day as it is. How do I add this to my life without it affecting something else?

I would definitely expect it to affect your current life. If you are having a hard time even considering an hour a day, then you are not that serious about overcoming your fear of public speaking. That's the old you talking, and he is trying hard to find reasons to keep things the way they are.

The old you will say anything to make sure life doesn't change. Change is typically uncomfortable for most people, especially change that puts a strain on our current comfort level. However, we cannot grow within the confines of a routine because nothing changes. If nothing changes, our lives are stagnant. I'm not saying routines are bad, but we can't expect things to change within a routine, and it would be insanity to think otherwise.

My question to you is, "Is it worth it?" Is it honestly worth living in fear and living with anxiety over speaking in public if you don't have to?

Would you not gladly dedicate an hour a day to relieve yourself of your fears and stressors that do nothing but cause you unnecessary grief and hold you back from your true potential? Why settle for a second-class version of yourself if you already have what it takes to become a better you? The only thing stepping in the way of your better self is time and effort. Those are small prices to pay for what's ahead.

So choose to change. Choose to take the risk and face your fears daily.

Fear will either hinder you, or it will simply be an obstacle. Your choice. Fear will stop you from asking for a raise even if you know you're worth it and deserve it.

Fear will stop you dead in your tracks when all you want to do is ask that cute girl in your office building out on a date.

Fear will stop you from taking a chance on a business opportunity.

Fear will cut you down when all you want to do is seek employment elsewhere from that dead end job.

Fear will hold you back from running for a leadership position in the committee you're involved in.

Fear will stop you from even trying.

Fear will either stop you or make you a better person. The choice is 100% yours, but only if you take responsibility for your life. The moment you don't take responsibility for your life is the moment you give your choice to someone or something else.

Imagine facing one of the decisions mentioned above after a year of speaking in public once a week and practicing daily. Take asking for a raise, for example: That nervous feeling in your stomach as you walk toward your boss's office is far from foreign to you by now. It's that feeling of approaching what you are afraid of instead of running from it. By now you've built up a tolerance to it.

You've grown to live with it, and even use it to perform at your best as your body releases small doses of adrenaline to keep you at your peak performance. This feeling isn't new to you. The old you might peek his head in and whisper, "what if. . ." before walking into the boss's office, but you have heard that song so many times now that you drive in without slowing your pace. You step through the threshold and take a moment to think back one year's time and realize how far you've come.

Without that practice, you might have chosen to never try and ask for that raise. You might have convinced yourself that now is not a good time. There's just too many emails to respond to and too much work to get done. You'll just wait until things slow down.

But you do have that practice behind you, and you can face your fears head on and ask for that raise.

Even after understanding the importance of committing this time, it can still seem daunting. Just realize you can get creative. Most of the tasks throughout the week can be done during a lunch break. You can even rehearse your speech during your commute to and from work or while running errands.

If I'm waiting in a public place for whatever reason and I have time to rehearse, I will rehearse. However, just so I don't get weird looks for "talking to myself," I'll pull out my phone and act as though I'm talking to someone. I'll even visualize myself in front of the crowd if I'm just sitting around doing nothing.

You: Can I just do all of this the day before if I have the time?

Yes, it's definitely possible but you will be missing out on the most important aspect of this approach: daily and consistent practice. Doing everything the day before prevents you from making public speaking, and ultimately facing your fears, a part of your daily life.

Working every day toward your goal of facing your fears has far more benefits in the sense of growth dividends compared to simply preparing only the day before. Also, if something comes up the day before and you can't get everything done, you've put yourself in an awful situation of going in blind so to speak.

CHAPTER 22

START YOUR PLAN
WITH AFFIRMATIONS

Now that you are committed and ready, let's get into the real meat of our plan. I want to warn you that a plan is only good if you actually put it into action. If you don't actually follow through because of [insert excuse here], then everything prior to this is wasted.

You have to commit to follow through with action prior to writing your plan. It's too easy to feel like you accomplished something just by spending the time to make a plan. But having a plan is negligible compared to what you gain from taking the first step. So make a firm commitment now before we get started. Say the following out loud:

I, [state your name], commit to put my plan into action. I know a plan without action is useless, and *doing* is far greater than *planning*.

Now if you just read over that and didn't verbalize it, then hike your eyes back up there and let's try that again. You're only cheating yourself. Say it out loud a few times even. If you did read out loud the first time, then move on.

Verbalizing your plan is just as important as rehearsing your speech out loud. If you just rehearse it in your head, you will not perform as well. Rehearsing out loud also adds sensory data to your memory and experience, causing you to focus on the pronunciation of every word and actually hear what you are saying. These additional steps add more layers of information to your practice and have a greater effect on your memory due to the increased feedback.

That's the importance of saying the above statement out loud because the impact is far greater and has a better chance of sticking in your mental capacity versus just reading it in your head. For good measure, let's say it out loud one more time. If you want to add fuel to the fire, say it with conviction.

I, [state your name], commit to put my plan into action. I know a plan without action is useless, and *doing* is far greater than *planning*.

With that out of the way, plan for your plan to suck. It will most likely change. Every plan seems perfect until you put it into action because plans hardly ever match reality. We'll do our best to make our plan to speak once a week, but it's better to know ahead of time that things will not always go accordingly.

Life happens and you might not get to practice like you planned, or speak every single week, or you name it. Expect this to happen ahead of time so you don't get blindsided or discouraged and end up giving up. Every plan will face bumps, bruises, and obstacles, but remember those are simply life's way of giving feedback.

It's time to write down a plan. Go ahead and grab something to write with and write on. I'll wait.

You're ready? Cool. At the top, write "Speaking Plan." Right under that, write down the following affirmation that you will recite once in the morning and in the evening before bed:

"From now on, I will be on the hunt for opportunities to speak. No longer will I run away when an opportunity crosses my path, letting fear and my coward-self win. When opportunity knocks on my door, I will immediately say, "Yes!" before my old, coward self has a chance to scream, "No!" Throughout the day, I will continuously remind myself 'I, [state your name], will become a courageous speaker.'"

Now affirmations are one of those weird things that shouldn't work, but they do . . . internally at least. It's not like you can continuously tell yourself, "I'm going to be a millionaire. I'm going to be a millionaire. I'm going to be a millionaire," and the world will bend toward your will to make that a reality. The world doesn't change because of what you tell yourself, but *your* world certainly can because you are choosing what is important in *your* world.

This is a form of reticular activation—a small portion of the brain that acts like a night club bouncer responsible for letting important information in and keeping the unimportant information out. For example, when you're in a crowded room and everyone's talking to one another, you can't make out what anyone in particular is saying, but out of the white noise, you can hear someone say your name. Why? Because your name is the most important word in *your* world. You've already deemed that word important so picking that out of the noise is actually a no-brainer.

That's kind of how affirmations work. Continuously telling yourself "I will hunt down and seek out opportunities to speak throughout my day" does not automatically create opportunities. This simply changes the lens you see your life through. Opportunities now become important, and your brain will stop filtering them out.

As you start to do this, opportunities will seemingly pop out of nowhere, but they were always there to begin with. There's just a high chance you weren't looking for them. In reality, you were probably avoiding them.

The second portion of the affirmation will be your daily mantra: "I, [state your name], will become a courageous speaker." Say this out loud three times in a row every time you say it.

At first, you may forget to say it throughout the day, but it will soon become a normal part of your day. I've used several methods to help me remember, and the best way is to have a reminder that grabs your attention throughout the day. I've taken a plastic duck and taped it to a pen I use in my office. Every time I go to use it I ask myself, "Why did I do that? Why did I tape a duck to this pen?" That's when I remember to say my affirmations. Sounds ridiculous, but ridiculous is what I needed to prevent my brain from filtering out my reminder. Use whatever you need to help you remember throughout the day.

I also like to tape my morning affirmation to my car's steering wheel and on my bathroom mirror so I have no choice but to see it and remember to say my affirmation.

You: I'm game with looking for opportunities, but I'm still not seeing the point of telling myself I will become a courageous speaker. Seems pointless to me.

It would probably help to let you in on a little secret. You already use affirmations. You've been using them for a long time. However, they've most likely been negative affirmations. Little lies you tell yourself that you have gradually started to believe. These lies don't serve you. They feed your lesser self. Some of the following negative affirmations you might know all too well:

"I'm just not good enough to speak and probably never will be."

"I'm not talented like other speakers."

"No one cares what I have to say."

"There's no point trying because I'm not going to get any better."

"I always screw up and make mistakes in front of a crowd."

"I am a failure."

If you tell yourself something long enough, you are not only going to start believing the lie, but your brain will notice incidents supporting your beliefs and filter out anything contrary to your worldview.

It's been said that our attitude, expectations, and outlook on life are directly affected by the accumulation of our thoughts. If our thoughts are just riddled with negative affirmations about how much we suck at public speaking and how there's no changing that "fact," then is it hard to believe our thoughts could change or manipulate the way we approach public speaking, but they can.

Since our thoughts have such an effect on our lives, why not use them to our advantage to punch our fears in the face? Why not make them positive and empowering thoughts that better serve ourselves? We've already talked about how the words we use are important. Now we're going to use our thoughts to push us forward to look for opportunities to speak instead of holding us back.

Speaking of looking for opportunities to speak. . .

CHAPTER 23

ON THE HUNT

With our thoughts in check, after stating our affirmation out loud, we are now on the hunt for opportunities to speak. Any experienced hunter will hunt in locations that increase their odds. If deer is on the menu, then the woods is the place to be, and probably a section of woods where deer have been spotted before.

We'll take the same approach while looking for an opportunity to speak. We'll start by looking in places where people speak regularly.

Toastmasters

First things first, let's hop on our handy dandy laptop or smartphone and look up local Toastmasters' clubs in our area. I mentioned Toastmasters earlier in the book, so I'll briefly explain what it is for those who don't know. Toastmasters is an international club where members gather weekly to give prepared speeches or short, unprepared speeches called table topics for the sole purpose of developing its members into great and confident communicators and leaders. Toastmasters also hosts several speech competitions throughout the year, which is a phenomenal arena to supercharge our path to becoming a courageous speaker. If the idea of competing scares the poop out of you, that might be a great sign that competing is exactly something you should considering doing.

Toastmasters can become a one-stop shop to satisfy our one speech a week requirement. It is one of the only places where your audience is there to help you succeed because they are there for the same reason you are: to become a better speaker. It's a safe environment to practice, make mistakes, and get better on a weekly basis.

Keep in mind Toastmasters is not free. Now, before you put the padlock on your wallet, I'm here to tell you it's beyond worth it. While I'm a frugal guy who typically cringes at spending anything over $5 on non-essential items, especially on something such as a club membership, this investment has been well worth it.

It is only $50 for six months. That's less than $10 a month to be among a group of people helping me punch my fears in the face and willingly be my audience every week. That's a bargain, and the value is priceless.

Some of us have spent thousands on furthering our education and most of us spend more than Toastmasters' fees with a few visits to Starbucks. The money is negligible compared to what you can get out of it.

While there are other places to hunt for opportunities, this is my first go to source. I simply shoot an email to the VP of our club requesting to speak at the upcoming club meeting. If there is an opening, I've got my speaking gig lined up for the week.

With regards to competing, winning at each level (club, area, and division) allows you to keep competing all the way to district, guaranteeing you have to give a speech every week as you are either competing or practicing at the weekly club meetings. The first competition I competed in gave me eight weeks of speaking opportunities. Not bad.

I hope by now I've got you seeing the value in Toastmasters because now you need to find a local club near where you live or work. This can be as simple as going on www.meetup.com and searching "Toastmasters" or going on www.toastmasters.org and finding a club near you.

You: Well Cody, I looked, and there isn't a club around me for 100 miles. What do I do now?

You've got two options: start your own Toastmasters club in your area or look someplace else to speak weekly. Starting a club in your area is a tough task, but that alone can supercharge your ability to speak as well as further your leadership abilities. The scope of that is beyond the context of this book, but don't let that discourage you from considering starting a club.

For the rest of our time in this section, I will show you plenty of other places you can give your weekly speech.

Work

Just look where you spend the better part of your day: work. Odds are in your favor that you will have opportunities to speak there. After all, there's bound to be annual or monthly training everyone has to take. There is safety training, ethics training, so on and so on. The trainings never seem to end or so it seems. That's great news for you! Someone has to instruct or teach those trainings and, most likely, a poor soul just got assigned this extra duty. If that's the case, then they would be more than willing to give that additional duty to you if you request it.

Most job sites also have newcomers' orientation, requiring someone in the company to brief new employees on what to expect while on the job. This is another great opportunity to speak.

I took full advantage of the opportunity to speak through my job. I signed up to teach resiliency training for my directorate.

Everyone I work with is required to attend four one-hour long resiliency trainings each year. The trainings cover twelve different topics. With this, I was guaranteed an audience, 10-30 people, whenever I scheduled a class.

Outside of the key resiliency material I had to teach, I could instruct my classes however I pleased, which meant I could practice engaging my audience. What got them excited? What made them all turn into serial introverts? What would catch their attention? What would bore them to death?

As I found ways to engage and connect with the class, I made some mistakes, but I learned new things along the way.

These are my first options. If Toastmasters and work are not providing a chance to speak, I'll look elsewhere. Sometimes you don't have to look too far.

Church

If you happen to go to church, there are tons of opportunities to speak. You can lead a morning Bible study. Teach a Sunday school lesson to children. Give the service prayer before or after the sermon. My church has an individual speaker at the end of a Sunday sermon to give a weekly status of events and things to come over the next couple of weeks.

Guest Speaker

Lori Byron over at www.famousinyourfield.com got me thinking about being a guest speaker at different venues in my own community. She wrote a fantastic blog post (www.famousinyourfield.com/17-ways-to-find-speaking-opportunities/) on finding more opportunities to speak as a guest speaker which is something I wish I had sought after sooner. My top two favorite from her post are the following:

1) Most communities have local Rotary Clubs, Chamber of Commerce, and Young Professional Organizations. All of these groups need speakers for their weekly or monthly meetings throughout the year. So find someone you know who is a member and ask them if their group is looking for speakers and what topics they typically look for.

2) Odds are in your favor that a college, university, or even technical centers are close to where you live. Some professors or instructors love having guest speakers come in and talk to their class on a related subject. Are you an accountant in your local community? Try teaming up with a professor for an accounting class and talk to the students about what you do and new trends you are seeing in the industry.

Common Interest Groups

Have an interest or hobby you love to talk about? Are you into bee keeping? Needlepoint? Programming phone apps? Do you have some mad nunchuck skills? If so, then do a google search or check in with social media accounts to find groups with similar interests near you and volunteer to speak to the group. This will be an easy talk to put together since you have an interest in the topic.

Network

Reach out to your network to find more opportunities to speak. Post on Facebook if anyone knows of an opportunity to speak. Ask your boss, your pastor, or your community leaders the same thing. Be genuine in your request by telling them exactly what you're doing by looking for opportunities to become a better speaker by punching your fears in the throat. People are more open when you can be upfront about your intentions.

Improv Groups

To supercharge my growth, I'll look for opportunities to speak or perform on stage in front of an audience where I can't prepare ahead of time what I'm going to say or do. I'm forced to think on my feet.

I mentioned before that Toastmasters has 2 minute table topics where you are given a random topic to speak on for—you guessed it—2 minutes.

I also like to go on www.meetup.com and look up local improv groups that meet up on weekends. Originally, I never considered joining an improv/acting group. However, one week over the summer, I didn't have a chance to speak at all, so I figured I'd do a little google search.

I couldn't really find anything that I would typically go to, but a local improv group caught my attention. The thoughts of improvisation actually made me feel uncomfortable. I was actually a little afraid to show up and give it a shot—so that's exactly what I did. I showed up and gave it a shot ☺. It was great, I had fun, and it got me out of my comfort zone.

Create your own opportunities

There's no reason you cannot create opportunities to speak for yourself. If starting a Toastmasters Club seems too daunting, then go on to meetup.com and start a casual public speaking group in your community. There are bound to be more people looking for a place to become a better speaker. You can be the person to create it. If anything, you could create a group that meets at work in the mornings or during lunch for the sole purpose of improving everyone's public speaking skills.

Do you like board games? Did you know there is a board game to help you improve your public speaking? Two of my fellow Toastmasters, Florian Mueck and John Zimmer, actually developed and manufactured a public-speaking game called *Rhetoric – The Public Speaking Game* that also comes in an app version. The board game itself is a little on the pricey end, and it has to ship from Europe. Luckily the app is only $6.99 as of writing this, which is a great price to have a fun time hanging out with friends and improving your public speaking at the same time.

—Cody's Note—

If you are considering purchasing the physical board game, you can reach out to the creators here: www.rhetoricgame.com.

Remember, you are looking for one opportunity to speak each week. Shoot for speaking for at least five minutes and try to find speaking opportunities that require you to prepare a speech ahead of time.

Speaking once a week is the goal, but life happens so don't fret too much. If a week or two goes by, and you haven't had the chance to speak just make sure you are consistently saying your affirmation and always on the lookout for opportunities.

Your opportunities can come from a combination of what I've mentioned above, which is certainly not an all-inclusive list by any means. From Toastmasters, work, Church, volunteering, and your network, you are very likely to find opportunities to speak.

Now add to your plan, writing down at least five places you could look for opportunities to speak. Let those be your hunting ground. Now go out there and look for opportunities, ask for opportunities, and shoot, create some if you have to. Before you know it you'll have more than you know what to do with.

Get ready to accept . . .

CHAPTER 24

WHEN OPPORTUNITY KNOCKS

When you are on the hunt for an opportunity to speak and an opportunity presents itself, typically, you would think about the opportunity then act on it afterwards. However, that creates too much time for your coward self (the old you) to interject with a mountain of reasons why you can't or shouldn't take them up on the opportunity to speak.

While you are in the middle of mentally flipping through your calendar, your old self will chime in with something like:

"That's just another thing to add to my plate, and I'm busy as it is."

"8 P.M.?? That's way too late in the night to speak! Especially on a weeknight!"

"There is someone else who could speak on this better than me."

The comments will be never ending, and the more time you take to think about it, the more uncomfortable you will feel, and the more likely you will decline the opportunity.

I want you to be hungry for an opportunity to speak and jump for it like it's a cheeseburger, and you haven't eaten for eight days (or a pile of kale if you're vegan). I want you to accept before your coward self has time to even know what hit him.

You want to stop going to a place of fear and stress when an opportunity presents itself, but instead go immediately to a place of excitement.

This is why the morning affirmation is so important! Reading it out loud in the morning sets the tone for the day. Instead of falling into the same trap of avoiding and declining a chance to speak, you are now telling yourself (with conviction!) to look for a chance to speak first thing in the morning. Don't forget about your daily mantra to become a courageous speaker. A courageous speaker jumps at an opportunity to speak even if the opportunity is terrifying. A courageous speaker does NOT listen to their coward self and the laundry list of reasons why they should run like hell instead.

You: "But what if I accept an opportunity to speak, but later realize I truly can't due to circumstances outside of my control?"

I would rather have you politely decline after accepting than to take time to think about the opportunity and eventually talk yourself out of it. If you TRULY have circumstances outside of your control that prevent you from speaking, then that's perfectly understandable

However, if the reason you cannot speak has a flavor of inconvenience, or not making time for it, or not feeling comfortable, then that's just making excuses.

I've fallen into this trap myself. Many times I've had to have some serious talks with myself about why I couldn't speak. I've found myself coming up with some pretty lame excuses that I truly wanted to believe were outside of my control, but they were not.

I didn't want to accept that I was the one making the decision to be a coward. Accepting that would mean having to take responsibility for my actions or inaction in this case. Looking deeper, my excuses all stemmed from my fears. I have worked to overcome that, and you need to too. Choose to say "yes" rather than "no."

Once you get in that habit, I would love to say your coward self crawls back into his cave and shuts up, but that is typically far from reality. Your acceptance will most like come across as disrespect to His Lowliness, The Coward King.

"What were you thinking!?" the Coward King yells as soon as he receives word you betrayed him. The answer, of course, is you were not thinking at all for once. An opportunity came knocking, and finally you opened the door without giving it a second thought.

But now the lowly king will feel blindsided, furious even, and he'll do whatever is in his power to make you second guess what you've just done. Even going as low as bringing up past memories of your "failures" speaking in front of an audience, but luckily you have already addressed those memories by turning those failures and mistakes into lessons. The Coward King will be furious, but he will eventually grow tired, give up and become silent.

Every now and then leading up to the time for you to speak, he'll try again to convince you to retreat. Change is hard, but stay strong. Expect the Coward King to speak up, and it won't catch you by surprise. It will get easier and easier to recognize his voice in your head, which in turn will make it easier to tune him out.

CHAPTER 25

I SAID YES, NOW WHAT??

If you have a speaking opportunity coming up, it's now time to prepare for your big speech. So you're going to use the other six days of the week to prepare and use as your playground to hone your skills.

If on Wednesday, you scheduled to speak next Tuesday then consider Wednesday day one.

Keep in mind this plan assumes you have at least seven days to prep for your speech. If you have more time to prepare, ranging greater than two weeks, I highly encourage you to find more opportunities to speak in the coming weeks prior to the opportunity at hand.

If you can't find another chance to speak, your once a week goal can be easily accomplished by simply preparing as if your speech is only 7 days away. For example, if you have two weeks between now and when you actually speak, go through the steps we are about to address during the first week, and at the end of the week, speak in front of friends, family, and/or co-workers as a dry run. Gather feedback from your practice audience, incorporate any needed improvements in yourself or your speech content, and then use the following week to simply practice giving your speech daily leading up until your actual speech day.

However, if your speech is greater than 30 minutes, then use all two weeks to work on it rather than the dry run method. It is still possible to properly prepare within six days, but your goal is to minimize the amount of time needed to prepare each day. If your speech requires more time to prep, then you will simply repeat days two through four until the last two days prior to speaking.

—Cody's Note—

If you have less than a week to prepare, then skip to chapter 28 where I talk about what to do in those situations.

DAY 1

On day one, you need to get your act together. If you don't already know your topic, then that's step #1. Most speaking events at work or in community involvement will give a good idea of the topic.

However, your speech might be for a public speaking group like Toastmasters or a local meet-up where the topic of your speech is completely up to you, and you'll have to start from scratch.

After deciding on the topic, you will spend the first day creating content, structuring your speech, and creating a rough draft.

Note: If you already have prepared content for your speech, skip to day two.

Be sure to carve out an hour of your day to complete the following steps:

Step 1: Know your topic

Step 2: Mind map

Step 3: Outline your speech

Step 4: Rough draft

Step 1: Know Your Topic

Note: If you already know your topic but need content, skip this step.

Try not to take more than 10 minutes to come up with a topic. Choose something you have experience with or a personal story you can connect to the topic. Having a story will make it easier to come up with content, though this is not essential.

Remember, our goal is not to deliver superior content, awe our audience, nor to be remembered as a legendary orator. All those things are great, worthy goals. However, we are working towards overcoming our fears and becoming more and more comfortable in front of a crowd. It truly doesn't matter how superior your content is if you are terrified to speak. The goal is to have the courage to get in front of a crowd. Keep that in mind and don't put too much pressure on finding the perfect topic.

With that in mind, let's say you looked around the room and noticed a bowl of fruit, particularly a bundle of delicious looking bananas, and you thought to yourself, "Boy, do I love bananas." Then choose bananas as your topic. Step 1 complete. Nailed it.

Yes, I realize this is an extreme case of truly not caring what your topic is, but let's roll with it.

Step 2: Mind Mapping

You might remember mind-mapping from grade school: you wrote your topic in the middle and branched off that topic to connect and write down everything you could think of. This is used a lot as a brainstorming activity to help you get everything out of your brain and onto paper. It's going to look messy, but messy is fine.

Now I want you to do this with me. Take no longer than 10 minutes and begin creating a mind map for the bananas topic.

If you haven't done this before or haven't for a long time, I'd like to share with you some expert level advice: write down ANYTHING that comes to mind and don't hold anything back. Your mind naturally starts judging or filtering thoughts as you go through the exercise because they seem silly or unrelated or stupid. All ideas are good ideas. Any thought that comes to your mind might not seem related or useful, but write it down anyway because that thought might spur a connection to something else related or useful, or remind you of a past experience/memory that will open up a whole gambit of content to speak on.

When you are ready, get out a blank sheet of paper and get to mind mapping! Try not to take more than 10 minutes.

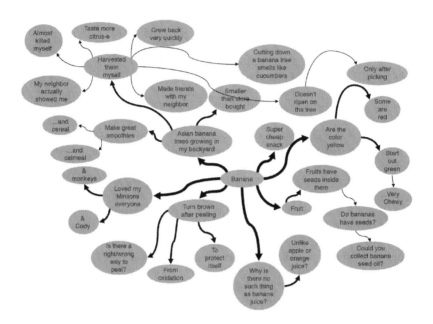

As you can see from my example, I have main branches off the main topic, and then I have even more branches off those main branches as I went through the exercise. This took me a grand total of four minutes to complete, and I had enough to talk about for at least 20 minutes. Luckily, we only need 5–7 minutes of content. With just four minutes of effort, I have more than I need. Now that's a good problem to have.

Don't be discouraged if it takes you longer to complete your mind map. Like all things, public speaking included, it gets easier with practice.

As you can see from my mind map, I wrote everything that came to mind. I wrote down things as simple as bananas are the color yellow, which spurred on more branches about how they start out green and how they don't actually ripen on the tree but only ripen after picking. Bananas also reminded me of the Minions from the animated movie *Despicable Me*.

The exercise led me to question why there isn't such a thing as banana juice or if bananas actually have seeds?

Going through this also reminded me of a time I had Asian Banana trees growing in my backyard that I harvested, which gave me even more mind-mapping material since I had a personal story to talk about.

Step 3: Outline Your Speech

In this step, you will convert your messy mind map into a less messy outline. The outline will become the structure or skeleton of our banana speech. I took some of my main branches and used them as my main subtopics. Anything that branched off my main branches, I wrote underneath as a subtopic and so on and so forth.

Banana Speech Outline:

1) Bananas are the color yellow
    1. Some are red
        1. Do they taste different?
    2. Start out green
        1. Very chewy when they are green
        2. Bananas don't actually ripen on the tree

    1. Only after picking off the tree
   3. Turn brown after peeling
     1. Due to oxidation
     2. To protect itself
     3. Is there a right and wrong way to peel a banana?
2) Bananas are a fruit
   1. Fruits have seeds inside them
   2. Do bananas have seeds?
     1. Is it possible to collect banana seed oil?
   3. Why is there no such thing as banana juice?
     1. Like apple and orange juice?
3) Story about my Asian Banana Trees
   1. Harvested them myself after my neighbor showed me how
     1. Tastes more citrus-ee than store bought
       1. Smaller too
       2. Great in smoothies/cereal/oatmeal
     2. Almost killed myself harvesting
       1. About fell off a ladder
     3. The trees grow back quickly
       1. The trees start to bleed when you cut them down
         1. The banana tree blood smells like cucumbers
           1. Very sticky and will stain your clothes
4) ETC
   1. Bananas are loved by Minions everywhere
     1. & Cody
     2. & monkeys
   2. Super cheap snack

After I converted everything over to my outline, I organized the topics in order.

This took me roughly 10 minutes to complete.

You might have noticed I added more under some of the subtopics than what was on my mind map. Converting my mind map over to my outline helped me remember even more content, so I wrote those new ideas down.

If you are a perfectionist, like myself, do your best to fight the urge to make your outline perfect from the get-go. Go ahead and convert your banana mind map over to your outline if you haven't already. This can be done on a different sheet of paper or on the back of the sheet of paper you wrote your mind map on.

Step 4: Rough Draft

There are several ways to write your rough draft. One method can save you time: use a computer to convert what you say into text. There is some pretty expensive software out there that can do this for you . . . or you can do it for free ☺.

With your outline in front of you, complete these steps:

Step 1) Open up a web browser using *Chrome*.

Step 2) Go to www.google.com and type in: Web speech API Demonstration.

Step 3) Open the "Web Speech API Demonstration - Google" link.

Step 4) Click the microphone icon on the next screen and just simply start speaking on your topic, using your outline to guide you.

> **—Cody's Note—**
>
> **You can also insert punctuation using your voice: say "Period" or "Comma" to insert those marks or say "New paragraph" to go to a new paragraph.**

Again, don't try and make it perfect the first go around. Just speak because this is a draft, not a final product. Consider it more of a prototype.

The reason this is so effective is because we can speak SO MUCH faster than we can type or write free hand. It won't be even close to perfect, but you can edit later. Cut yourself some slack and get to speaking!

This took me roughly 10 minutes to open up a web browser and talk through my entire outline. 10 minutes and BOOM! My rough draft is complete!

I'll take a few more minutes to make soft edits if words are missing or if the software didn't pick up on a sentence or two. Other than that I'm done for the day.

All four steps should take less than an hour to complete, even if you have to type out and/or hand write your speech.

At this point, you haven't spoken a single word as far as practicing goes, and that's okay. If you try cramming more into your day, then it is easy to start associating practice, preparing, and learning with a lot of time and effort. Once that happens, Netflix starts looking even more enticing compared to practicing.

Don't get me wrong: it is a lot of time and effort. Here, in the Stage Fight Club, we don't believe in lying, and I'm not going to start lying to you. Since you made it this far into the book (I congratulate you for getting this far!), you already know and accept that it does take a lot of time and effort to overcome your fears. However, that doesn't mean you can't spread out that time and effort over a week.

With the rough draft complete, pat yourself on the back! You just got a lot of work done, and it's only day one. On Day two, you'll actually start practicing and editing your speech as it really starts to take shape.

DAY 2

Day two, you will actually begin rehearsing your speech. Just know that this will be a rough, rough draft. Some people want to try and perfect their speech on paper before actually doing a dry run.

If this is your first time going through this, you should have your banana rough draft ready to go.

Before you start, reassure yourself that you are working with a rough, rough draft of your speech. Reading through it, you may think "Good gracious this is horrible!" and you'll probably be right. In its current state, it is probably very bad, but I want you to remember that this is all part of the plan. The final will be much better. The speech you actually give to your audience compared to your draft will feel like night and day. With that mindset ready, let's begin.

Have your speech in front of you and speak every word from beginning to end. As you read, just make mental notes of the flow of your speech.

When you are done, speak through it again, and this time make written notes of choppy sentences, sections that need more clarity, sections that should probably be removed, and needed transitions to create better flow from one idea to the next.

I like to print out my draft and make edits with a red pen. I'll read through the draft several times, and each time, I'll pick up more and more that I want to change, edit, remove, or add to chisel away at my draft. I'll spend 20–40 minutes doing this. Saying it out loud helps you edit your draft and will start stimulating mental roots in your brain to help you memorize your speech.

After you are feeling more comfortable with your revised draft (it's still a draft so it should not be perfect!), you are ready to try and video record yourself on either your phone, digital camera, or laptop.

—Cody's Note—

If you don't have a way to record yourself, ask a friend who has a phone, camera, or laptop you can borrow for this part. If that simply is not possible, just practice giving your speech out loud in private a few times in front of a mirror.

With your recording device up and running, do your best to remember your content, but don't worry if you need to look at your written speech; this is all just practice.

If you mess up during your recording, try not to start over. Keep chugging along as if nothing happened. In front of an audience, you won't get the opportunity to just start over, so this is perfect practice to mess up and keep moving along as if nothing happened. Remember, your audience will not remember your mistakes.

Once you're done recording, watch yourself give your speech. It can be VERY uncomfortable to watch yourself. It certainly is for me even though I've done it hundreds of time. However, this will give you some of the best feedback you will ever receive. Most speakers don't do this, and it's a shame. This simple exercise reveals so much about ourselves that we don't even realize. For me, I noticed little quirks to indicate nervousness; incorrect pronunciations; and my voice trailing off at the end of sentences, making it hard for my audience to hear.

Watching yourself speak can be an uncomfortable eye opener, but a priceless way to learn and improve! Don't down play the importance of this step simply because it's awkward or uncomfortable.

As you are watching your recording ask yourself the following questions:

Are you smiling?

How's your tone of voice?

Do you have vocal variation or are you mostly monotone?

Did your speech flow smoothly from one topic to the next?

Did each topic have enough clarity to make sense to your audience who might not have the same knowledge or background as you?

What are your hands doing?

What does your body language say about how you are feeling?

Do you look uncomfortable?

Did you display signs of a nervous tick?

Write down what you could improve in a notebook. Reflect on how you did and what you could do better. I do this with all of my speeches, and even after doing this hundreds of times, I still find things I could do better.

Professionals, in any field, don't reach professional status because they know everything there is to know in their field. They become professionals because they never stopped learning and improving.

So don't feel discouraged if you find a lot to improve on and definitely don't expect to fix everything over night! For now, pick two or three things from your notes to focus on during the remainder of today's practice time. Continue to record, make notes, and then practice.

—Cody's Note—

If you already had content (like pre-made slides) for your speech, then complete day two twice: today and tomorrow. Try to practice without looking at your slides. Afterwards go through the other steps for Day 2: recording yourself, watching the recording, noting feedback, and then practice again.

DAY 3

Today give your speech in front of someone. That's right! Get ready to speak in front of a member of the human race. Again, if this is your first time, go get that banana speech we've been working on.

Practice once or twice by yourself after reviewing your three improvement areas as a refresher. Afterwards, find someone willing to listen to you. This can be a spouse, boyfriend, girlfriend, neighbor, stranger, friend, co-worker, etc. The who really doesn't matter as long as they are willing to provide honest feedback. If you are able (and want to add additional pressure), find a group of people to speak in front of.

After you get done speaking, ask what you could do to improve, and be ready to be open to any and all criticism. There really is no such thing as constructive or destructive criticism. There is only criticism. It is up to you to choose whether you will use it to your advantage in a constructive manner or let it destroy you. You, and only you, get to choose.

You: You really like ending thoughts with requiring me to choose between two options, don't you?

Yes. Yes I do. Thanks for interrupting me. Now where was I? Oh yeah. Write down the feedback preferably in the same place you wrote down your own feedback from the day before.

If they are willing to listen to you again, give it another shot and try to apply the new feedback on the spot. If not, no worries! Thank them for their time and advice, and call it a day.

DAY 4

Day four is feedback review day. You should have a lot of feedback by now. Go back and review everything you wrote down so far. Today you're going to focus on making adjustments to yourself and your speech.

Looking over your feedback, do you notice patterns of behavior that show up multiple times? Does the same section of your speech never come out as clear as you want it? Do you consistently look down at the ground while you speak? Do you say filler words like "um" and "uh" between sentences? Make note of what feedback you keep getting the most and work on improving those. These areas will be the biggest bang for your buck as far as noticeable improvement goes.

When I first started watching my recordings for feedback, I noticed I mumbled like a mad man. I would cram eight words into one, and I had no idea I was doing it. In my head everything sounded crystal clear, but that was not the case in reality.

I knew that was an area, among others, that I could work on and notice an incredible amount of improvement. So I made extra effort to pronounce each and every word when I spoke. I noticed when I was tired, nervous, or just feeling lazy, I would mumble more often. I didn't realize just how much people would ask me to repeat what I was saying. I figured I was talking fast or their hearing sucked.

Come to find out that was not the case. Putting in the extra effort to pronounce my words resulted in drastic improvements. Do the same things with your feedback reviews, and you'll notice the same.

Work on what needs the most attention, but don't go overboard trying to make it perfect. It won't be.

As for your content, add anything you need to add for clarity, take out anything that is not essential, and rearrange and tighten up the organization with transitions if needed. Make it good enough, put a bow on it, make it your final draft, and call it a night.

If you want, take a moment and think back to the first time you spoke through your rough draft compared to today. Feel proud with the incredible work you've done so far and just how much you've improved.

__DAY 5__

Rehearse the final draft of your speech twice then find a quiet place, if you can, for the next exercise. You are going to visualize giving your speech to an audience. Olympian athletes and top performers do this all the time.

Several researches have even published research combining weight lifting and visualizing. Half of the group in these studies actually lifted weights for a period of time while the other half did NOT lift weights and just visualized lifting weights. The result? BOTH groups showed muscle growth and were able to lift more by the end of the study. That's incredible! That study showed the brain simply doesn't know the difference between reality and what we visualize. The bodily response was the same.

We'll use that trick to our advantage with public speaking. You ready?! Start by closing your eyes and visualize where you are going to be right before you speak. Your goal is to create a virtual reality of sorts by adding as much detail as you possibly can to the experience. The more details you have the better the results.

Do you know where you will speak? Visualize that place and where you might be right before you speak. If you don't know, simply imagine to the best of your ability. Is the speech indoors? Outdoors? Are you giving the speech in the morning? Late at night? What's the weather like? What are you wearing? A suit? Casual clothes? Are you on a stage? Standing at the far end of a conference table? What is your audience like? Children? Adults? How many people do you expect?

Bring all of these details into play to make it feel real to you. If you start to feel a little nervous (or really nervous) as if you are really about to speak in front of a crowd, then you are on the right track! This is the exact response we are looking for as it helps expand your tolerance for feeling uncomfortable, especially since your brain can't tell the different between visualizing and reality.

Imagine you are just about to speak, and you feel your nerves creep up on you, but you can keep them under control as you remember your nerves are just signaling this is important to you.

Picture yourself smiling and actually excited to speak. You know this is exactly where you need to be to grow as a speaker. You feel confident because you've practiced and practiced your speech more than you can count.

Imagine you can hear, and even feel, the size of the crowd around you. You know they are just as human as you are and probably just as afraid to speak in front of a crowd. Maybe even more afraid than you are in that moment.

Now imagine you've just been called to speak, and you can feel your heart pounding harder, but you are not turning back. Your heart is ramping up, but you are in control. You breathe slowly and stand tall and confident as you make eye contact with the crowd.

Imagine taking one more deep breath while scanning the crowd in front of you (actually take a deep breath while visualizing). As soon as you can't consume another molecule of air, smile and exhale your first few words of your speech. Actually speak out loud while keeping your eyes closed and visualizing the crowd. Go through your entire speech from start to finish.

Once you are done with your speech, keep visualizing that moment. Notice the feeling you feel as you realize you faced your fears and you had nothing to be afraid of.

Open your eyes and take a moment to note how your feel. Is there a sense of relief? Is your heart beating a little faster? Did your body release a dose of adrenaline?

Simply take a mental note and get ready to do it again. Try and add in even more details this time, and make the audience even bigger! Double or triple the amount of people you're speaking in front of. Now go through the exercise again. Keep doing this for whatever time you have allotted yourself. When you are done, call it a day.

DAY 6

It's the day before you will speak. Today you want to bust through a few practice rounds of your speech. Shoot for three rounds, and then you are close to calling it a night. After practicing and writing down any additional feedback you want to capture, it's time to write down your game plan for Day 7—Speech Day.

Your game plan outlines what you will do that day, starting with the moment you wake up. Actually it starts the night before, but we'll get into that. Get out a piece of paper and something to write with.

To help you mentally see the amount of time you have to prepare, note when you speak and when you wake up.

You will also want to note where you will speak so you can plan for how much time you need to get there. As an example, I've filled in information as if you were going to give your banana speech to a Toastmasters club.

When: 5:30 pm

Where: Toastmasters club meeting at the local library

Wake up time: 7:00 am

In this example, you would have roughly 10.5 hours in between the moment your eyes open, and the moment you say the first word of your speech. Now ask yourself, "Does this give me enough time to squeeze in a handful of quick activities to prepare me for my speech along with everything else I had planned to get done that day?" If it does, great! Move on to the next section where we'll talk about said activities. If not, now is a good time to prioritize.

Either wake up earlier (which is not always a great idea if you are not used to getting up earlier), or do what you can to make room for some prep work prior to your speech.

Speech day activities:

- Drink a large glass of water as soon as you wake up

- Recite your affirmation

- Exercise

- Do something that makes you feel alive

- Do something silly

- Journal your thoughts

- Practice your speech

These activities are my modified version of Hal Elrod's *Miracle Morning* activities (another great book I recommend). Do you have to do every single activity? No. These are just my recommendations. All of them help prepare you for your speech in their own unique way. I don't always do all of them. Sometimes I just don't have the time. You might even modify this to fit your particular style of prepping for a speech.

On your plan beneath where you wrote your wake-up time, write the activities you will do today as a to-do list.

CHAPTER 26

SPEECH DAY ACTIVITIES

DRINK WATER

As soon as you wake up drink some water (12 oz at least). That's a typical bottle of water.

While you sleep, you lose water that you need to replenish. Odds are you wake up dehydrated and don't even know it. Our bodies, especially our brains, need proper/adequate amounts of water to function at peak performance. Plus, that water will help flush out the grogginess from waking up.

Time: 2 Minutes

AFFIRMATION

Since you're not hunting for a job opportunity today, your affirmation changes.

"Today, I am a courageous speaker. I am prepared, confident and ready to give my speech. Even though I am prepared, I give myself permission to suck. I am confident I will grow from this experience, and I am absolutely ready to punch my fears. IN. THE. FACE!"

TIME: ~1 Minute

EXERCISE

Next you need to exercise, preferably outside. Being outside wakes up your senses from the sounds you hear, what you see, the feel from the change in temperature, and the smells you smell. With your senses waking up, exercise helps wake up the rest of your body: your heart, your lungs, your muscles, your blood system, etc.

The exercise is up to you and can be as easy as a brisk walk for 10 minutes or so. You don't have to crank it up to CrossFit insanity, and don't make it any more intense than what you are used to. Flipping tractor tires for the first time the day of your speech is a recipe for disaster. The last thing you need is to overwork yourself or cause injury before you even have a chance to speak. Afterwards, you should feel much more awake and most likely feeling pretty good.

Take a shower afterwards if you need to. This is when I check off my activity that makes me feel alive.

Time: ~10 Minutes

DO SOMETHING THAT MAKES YOU FEEL ALIVE

I reward myself for exercising with a warm shower, but I end it with a freezing cold shower for about 30 seconds to a minute. The cold water shocks my body into existence. My heart races. My breathing is uncontrollable. Fight or flight kicks in, and I have to make a choice. Turn the shower back to warm, turn the shower off, or stick with it and fight it!

I choose to fight it, and soon fighting becomes embracing the cold shower. I can't help but send out a "WHOA!" as the water wakes up every cell in my body.

What feels like an eternity is really less than a minute in reality. Gradually, I start to control my breathing and my body starts to adapt. As I stop shaking, I think "This is actually okay. It doesn't matter if this continues or not because I'm going to be okay."

At that point, I end the shower. The water stops, and I feel amazing! Unstoppable even! I realized it's during those showers that I can't think of the past or the future. There is not a single worry, regret, or fear because I'm completely in the present.

You might find another way to feel alive whether that is listening to your favorite song, driving with the windows down to feel the wind, or stealing (seriously, don't do that last one). Whatever works and is readily available to fit into your day, do that!

I would highly recommend the cold shower because it's really hard to replicate that feeling, and it only takes less than a minute of your day. Secondly, just like with public speaking, you have to willingly choose to step into a place of discomfort (cold shower) while currently in a place of comfort (warm shower). You don't get that same effect listening to music or driving with the windows down because both of those situations don't create the mental barrier you must choose to break through.

Time: ~5 Minutes

Before we get into the other activities, do everything else that you usually do to start your day: get dressed for work, eat breakfast, get the kids ready for school, whatever. Get this stuff done so you're not thinking about what you need to do while doing the rest of your speech prep activities, which you can schedule at any time in the day.

REHEARSE YOUR SPEECH

Find some time in your day before you speak to rehearse your speech. If you can actually practice in the same place where you are expecting to speak, that's even better. Run through your speech a few times if you can, but know when to call it quits.

By now you've already practiced at least 15 times in the past week. Feel confident you've put in the necessary time and effort to properly prepare and feel assured you've put in more work than most speakers who might simply practice the night before or the morning of. Even if you still don't feel ready, remember that's just the old you talking. The new you has already given yourself permission to suck. You know by now sucking is the dues we pay to get better and grow.

Time: ~5–30 Minutes (depending on the length of your speech)

DO SOMETHING SILLY

Find some time to do something silly. This helps you to not take yourself so seriously, calms your nerves, and helps you to loosen up. Fear can strike a chord with our nerves that make us stiff and uptight. You need something to counteract that, and being silly, even borderline embarrassing, can do that. This can take a thousand different forms. If you think of doing something that makes you feel uncomfortable (yet legal) and causes you to smile, you should consider doing that. You are on the right track!

Below are a few things I've done. All of which my wife does not know about. Maybe she'll find out if she actually reads my book.

- Smiled at myself in a mirror for two minutes with the biggest, cheesiest grin on my face

- Went to McDonalds and ordered my food via singing. Lots of weird looks on this one.

- Danced in a Wal-Mart parking lot outside of my car while blaring a Taylor Swift song. I believe it was "Shake It Off."

- Went to a public bathroom (which I thought was empty) and practiced an evil laugh.

During that last one, someone in a stall asked in a really confused voice:

"Why are you doing that?"

His question scared the crap out of me (luckily, I was in a bathroom). I was already embarrassed, so I answered his question honestly.

"I have to give a speech, and I'm doing something silly to calm my nerves. . . ."

"Oh . . . that makes sense I guess. I get nervous too. Can I try?"

There was a bit of an awkward silence before I answered.

"Sure, why not."

At a certain point, it became a competition, and soon we started busting out laughing. The bathroom patron started stomping his feet from laughing, and I had to run to a urinal before I pissed in my pants. It turned out to be more than I needed to relax my nerves. I actually gave one of my better speeches that day. Thank you bathroom patron—whomever you are.

Spontaneous action is key here. If you think about it for too long, you'll most likely let the old you debate long enough to convince yourself not to.

Time: ~5 Minutes

—Cody's Note—

I've recently been experimenting with rejection therapy after reading *Rejection Proof* **by Jia Jiang. I've been using rejection as my "do something silly" activity before I speak, and I'm seeing great results. I highly recommend reading his book to learn more about rejection therapy. Life changing.**

JOURNAL YOUR THOUGHTS

I'll try and journal on a sheet of paper my thoughts about an hour before I go on stage, which is usually when I can feel my nerves get a little jumpy. I'll simply write down how I'm feeling and why, taking five minutes to write. I'll usually just write this down on my game plan paper. It's incredible how much clarity I can achieve in my mind by simply writing down how I feel and discovering why. If you do this, don't think about what you're going to write. Just write. It doesn't even have to be about how you're feeling.

Time ~5 Minutes

CONTROL YOUR NERVES

If at any point you start to feel your nerves get the better of yourself, plan to stop the fire before it spreads. What you choose to do can take many forms.

Whenever I feel my fear creeping up, I first recognize that I'm feeling nervous. This happens more frequently as the time between now and when I speak comes closer and closer. I'll take three deep, slow breathes as I visualize banishing my coward self back to his cave. I'll then ask myself (and answer) out loud the following questions:

Why am I afraid?

—Well . . . because I'm afraid to look like an idiot and not be accepted in front of a lot of people.

Is that something I'm willing to accept to grow?

—Yes, I'm willing to accept that.

Is my audience full of people who are also afraid of speaking in front of people?

—Most likely.

Is my audience made up of perfect, flawless people who've never made mistakes?

—Definitely not!

Is my audience going to remember my performance and every mistake I make forever and ever?

—Nope. They are most likely going to forget everything five minutes after I finish speaking because they (just like me) are more consumed with what's going on with their own lives than someone else's.

I'll then take three more deep, slow breathes, and during my exhale, I'll wish my audience happiness. Wishing my audience happiness gets my mind off of myself and my nerves.

Lastly, I'll do something active like go for a brisk walk, do pushups, or squats. Something to keep me active, and I'll keep a huge grin on my face while I do it. That is my ritual, and I might do this a few times during the day, depending on how nervous I am. I'll even go through this ritual if I can right before I speak.

Time: ~10 Minutes

THAT'S IT!

That's the game plan in a nutshell. The only other thing I like to do before I speak is find someone (usually someone I know) who can either record me giving my speech or at least pay close attention to my performance and later give me feedback.

If I simply just ask someone afterwards how I did without giving them the task beforehand, I've noticed I hardly get any feedback at all. That made me realize just how little people pay close attention or even notice any of my mistakes or flaws, which should come to you as a relief rather than a disappointment.

That's your full week at a glance. You'll be impressed how far you will improve from day one mind mapping versus your performance on the day you speak. Work pays off in the long run.

You: So do I have to do this every week from now on so I can control my fears?

Not necessarily. You'll start to really notice changes after 4–6 weeks of speaking once a week. After 3–4 months, you'll feel a greater sense of confidence and courage to really overcome your fears. At that point, you could easily go into maintenance mode by speaking twice a month.

I continue to speak at least once a week because I want to become a professional speaker, coach others, and eventually start speaking to bigger and bigger crowds to continue improving. I understand that for most people overcoming their fears is the ultimate goal, and they are completely comfortable stopping there.

SECTION 5

—

LESSONS LEARNED FROM MY PUBLIC SPEAKING EXPERIENCES

CHAPTER 27

SPEAK COURAGEOUSLY—
LIVE COURAGEOUSLY

January 2014—Mississippi State University

Facing my public speaking fears led to great opportunities for me such as starting a business in college with one of my fraternity brothers, Daniel.

On a snowboarding trip with our fraternity, we played games almost every night. On our way home, we decided to make our own game where you used the cards to "build" a robot, and once that robot was complete, you would battle the other players. Last robot standing wins.

We spent the first half of that next school semester creating our game. We made the first cards on flashcards (drawn by yours truly ☺). The artwork was horrendous, and the rules were not flushed out well. Slowly, after having fraternity brothers and other students test our game, Beep Boop, we had a game people found fun and might actually be willing to pay for.

Even with a fun game, that didn't change the fact that we were typical, poor college students without a lot of money to spare to support a business, let alone buy pizza on weekends. We needed funding to get it off the ground. Searching around led us to the Entrepreneurship Club, also known as the E Club, on campus within the business college.

It was there we learned about the Entrepreneurship Center (E Center) where they held a monthly board meeting allowing students to pitch their business ideas and the board chose whether to grant them seed money. We contacted them and scheduled our presentation for April and decided to attend the March meeting to get a feel for it.

Daniel and I met up in the business college before walking into the board meeting. My expectations were thrown out the window when I walked in the room. For whatever reason, I thought the desks would be in a circle like a classroom, and we wouldn't even have to stand in front of the room to pitch. I was completely wrong.

The room arranged with a long conference room table that seated over 20 people. The members of the board were seasoned business college professors, and the idea of facing a straight line of 20 of them felt like standing before a firing squad. It was terrifying.

Several students, well-dressed but noticeably nervous, made their way into the room. The board director made a few opening remarks, and one by one the students pitched their ideas. Some merely had ideas starting from scratch while others had existing businesses currently making a profit.

Once the students were done with their pitch, the questions began, and some of them were hard to answer. They would ask about their competitors, target market, price of production, and where were they going to manufacture their product. Their questions would point out the flaws in the business plan.

Daniel and I hardly had a business plan at all. Our plan was to make the game, sell the game, rinse and repeat.

Daniel took notes while I sat there stunned and afraid. My old self was coming up with reasons to not pitch at all.

My thoughts led to a downward spiral of doubt and fear. When Daniel bumped me with his elbow and said "This is intense, and it's also our chance to make Beep Boop a reality," he stopped the spiral, and I smiled back.

Was I really going to let my fear stop me from at least trying? I'd been working to overcome my fears for months by speaking to an audience once a week, and this was another great opportunity to do just that. I was not going to let my fear stop me from at least trying. The worst that could happen is we wouldn't get any money, and that seemed really small compared to everything else that was going on.

After thinking it through, I felt much better, and decided to take advantage of that meeting as best I could. When the meeting was over, Daniel and I stuck around and talked to some of the students who pitched, gaining valuable information before we pitched at next month's meeting.

We gathered what we learned, combined them with Daniel's notes, and used them to make a plan for the next 30 days. We put together a presentation and practiced our pitch by ourselves, in front of our fraternity brothers, and in front of experienced students working in the E Center.

It was easy to construe their feedback as personal attacks on my flaws instead of areas to improve. I had to continuously remind myself that the feedback will make me better, recognizing I had a choice to see them as attacks or lessons. That decision is yours to make as well so choose wisely.

We adjusted our presentation (and ourselves) according to their feedback and continued practicing up until the next board meeting.

The day had come, my nerves were high, but I was keeping them in check. After opening remarks, the board called us up first, so Daniel and I took our places at the front of the conference table. The conference table looked like it went on forever from where we were standing.

Daniel began to speak, and I could feel a lump in my throat that I just couldn't swallow, but then my turn came to speak. As soon as I spoke the first word all of our practice kicked in, and I went into autopilot mode. I started to feel calmer and less stiff. We still ran into a few bumps and bruises, but we managed to recover and finish the pitch.

The pitch was over, and we could both breathe easy for a moment before the questions started. Since they asked questions we weren't expecting, we stumbled through answers, often saying "We had not thought of that; we'll have to get back to you next time . . ." if there was ever going to be a next time.

Afterwards, Daniel grinned at me and held out his fist. I smiled back and responded with the manliest fist bump ever known (you don't know, you weren't there). It felt great going through with it and not backing down.

That evening, we found out they granted us $500. It wasn't all we had requested, but it was $500 more than we had going into the meeting. It was definitely a start.

Over the next two years, Daniel and I pitched to the board several more times, giving updates and asking for more money. Each time we got significantly better at presenting and speaking, and each time, we received more and more grant money.

In between board meetings, we discovered entrepreneurship competitions that we could compete in for additional money. While these competitions were more intense in front of hundreds of people, we plowed through anyway, changing our tactics from presenting our plan to entertaining the crowd.

To entertain the crowd, you have to be fairly comfortable on stage; otherwise, your nervousness bleeds out into your audience, preventing you from loosening up and getting comfortable.

All the experience we had gained consistently pitching allowed us to do just that.

I began to notice I no longer feared public speaking, and I didn't have to convince myself but rather looked forward to it.

I still got nervous, but my nerves no longer got out of control.

Throughout college, we continually went in front of the E Center, giving updates and requesting more money. At the end of the year, we requested $3,000 for a Kickstarter campaign.

—Cody's Note—

As I write this, Beep Boop is finishing up mass production in China and is scheduled for shipment before the end of 2017.

We would never have been so bold to ask for that much money in front of the board had we not gone through and experienced all the public speaking experiences those past two years. It was from the continuous and consistent pursuit of speaking in front of an audience that allowed us to build up the courage and skills we needed in that moment. Without that, starting Beep Boop would not have been possible.

Motivated by my desire to help Beep Boop become a success, I wanted to get better at pitching my ideas, so I signed up to speak at a pitch competition that required myself and another student to come up with a solution to solve the issues people with severe arthritis had while trying to brush their teeth. We had to present our solution to the MSU E Center plus an audience of students.

This opportunity was well outside my comfort zone because I didn't have a lot of time to prepare (~two weeks), and Daniel was too busy that semester to compete.

My initial gut reaction was to decline, but I knew I would grow more from this since it made me so uncomfortable just thinking about competing with a new product. However, I found a partner, Tyler, and did it anyway.

After working hard to prepare, the day of the competition arrived. When we took our place on stage, we jumped into our pitch with all the energy and enthusiasm we could muster. We presented the "Nook & Cranny Toothbrush," and we hit them with our slogan.

Tyler: We've got the skills
Cody: To protect yo grills

It was silly and corny, but the crowd and the judges laughed and enjoyed it. Connecting with the audience in a way whether with humor, emotion, or credibility builds a layer of trust and comfort for you and your audience. For me, this has come with practice. At first I just wanted to gain control of myself on stage. As soon as I started feeling more comfortable in front of the crowd, the more I could loosen up, try new things, and read the room to better connect with my audience.

The judges took 20 minutes after everyone was done to determine the winner and to collect votes for crowd favorite.

Host: And the winner for the Toothbrush Design Pitch Competition is . . .

It's always in those moments I tend to get my hopes up. Who wouldn't? I had done enough of these to know the real reward was the courage you get from speaking in front of a crowd. The difference between who I was just a year prior to who I was sitting in that crowd waiting to hear the winner was night and day. I used to be a fish out of water on stage but now . . .

Host: Tyler and Cody with the Nook & Cranny Toothbrush!

The crowd applauded, and Tyler had to almost help me out of my chair because I couldn't believe it. I probably had a dumb look on my face from not quite knowing how to accept that much positive reinforcement. When we got to the stage, they gave us a giant check for $1,000, and my dumb self thought, "we're supposed to take that to the bank??"

—Cody's Note—

By the way, if you try to slide a 5 foot by 5 foot check across the counter to the bank teller, they won't cash it! ☺

Many doors opened up because we participated in that competition. We were asked to speak in front of other board meetings, and the E Center texted me personally asking if I would give an elevator pitch. Elevator pitch competitions only give you 60 seconds to speak, and I had nothing prepared. Despite all my experience speaking, my old, scared self really had the upper hand. I would have just texted back "Can't. Sorry." But I stopped and asked myself a series of powerful questions to ensure that my decision was not driven by fear and anxiety.

What am I afraid of?

—Embarrassing myself in front of hundreds of people.

Is that all that bad if that's the worst outcome?

—I guess not.

Good or bad will they forget about my performance shortly after?

—Most likely.

Do I have anything to gain from competing?

—Absolutely!

What do I have the gain?

—More experience competing under pressure.

—A chance to win additional cash.

—A chance to network with successful business owners.

—Opportunities and open doors I can't foresee that won't be available if I decide to decline.

Walking through those questions not only helped me calm my nerves, but ultimately helped me see the bigger picture. I texted back, "Sure!" I had to quickly take a 10 minute presentation and get it down to just 1 minute.

I cut everything that was nonessential and rehearsed over and over. It was not easy cutting information that I thought was needed, but the more I cut, the easier it was to remember, and the less words I had to cram into 60 seconds. Had I not I probably would have sounded like a chipmunk on black tar heroin trying to speed speak through my pitch.

When the time came, I could only clutch my hands together and look at my shoes as I whispered to myself, "Everything to gain, nothing to lose." I heard the applause which signaled the previous student had just finished. The host for the event gave a brief introduction about me and called me up. There was no stage, just an open area. I faced the audience after hitting my mark, took a deep breathe, smiled and gave it everything I had.

That minute flew by in an instant. Before I knew it, it was over, the crowd applauded, the judges asked a few questions, the crowd applauded again, and I took a seat. I waited to sober up from the adrenaline that was still coursing through my body.

My heart was still racing rapidly, but I felt great. Amazing actually. I sat there as the next competition started, and I just felt happy I decided to pitch. Competing was extremely uncomfortable but I grew the most from experiences just like that. I won third place, receiving $750.

I tell you all of this because public speaking has truly changed my life for the better. It can absolutely do the same for you. When you step outside your comfort zone by speaking in front of an audience, you make yourself vulnerable. You are exposed to the crowd and their judgment of your performance. You are also exposed to new opportunities, opening doors that would never have been available to you had you just been a member of the crowd. Opportunities you will never know existed unless you actually decide to take action, fight your fears, and speak.

—Cody's Note—

If you're looking for more information about Beep Boop or considering purchasing a copy to play with your friends, you can find out more at www.akimbogames.com

CHAPTER 28

WHEN YOU DON'T HAVE A LOT OF TIME TO PREPARE

Just like with that pitch opportunity I received over text, there may come a time where you might be given a chance to speak without a lot of time to prepare. I don't want you to decline just because there is not a decent amount of time to get ready.

I have been there, and you can do it. It is important that you rely on the seven principles to help you through those experiences.

One such experience came from my church.

August 1st, 2017

Every first Tuesday of the month, my church goes to a local homeless shelter and gives a sermon to those staying there for the night. On Sunday, July 30th after worship, the leader who coordinates the event walked up to me and asked frankly, "Do you want to speak at the next trip to Beacon Light Mission? We don't have anyone to speak this month."

I had never gone on one of the trips out to the homeless shelter. I didn't even know when or where I was going to speak, but I knew better than to start asking questions because my old self would immediately formulate excuses. Before I could even think about it, I said "yes."

After I accepted, Coward Cody (or CC as I like to call him) started asking questions since I didn't give him an opportunity to speak.

CC: What were you thinking?

Me: I was thinking this would be another great opportunity to speak.

CC: Great opportunity?! You don't even know what to expect or what you're going to talk about this Tuesday?

Me: You're right about that, but if I had taken the time to think about that, I probably would have listened to you and missed a great chance to better myself.

Coward Cody had nothing else to say, but he did make a great point. I had two days to prepare. It wasn't a lot of time to put a speech together, but that wasn't a big enough problem to consider it a bad thing.

I know the words I use affect my outlook. If I thought to myself "I *only* have two days to prepare," that would create a negative mental barrier I would have to deal with. Instead, I decided to spin it in a more positive light: "I have a full 54 hours between now (1 p.m. Sunday) and the moment I go on stage (7 p.m. Tuesday)." That felt like more than enough time.

It's not easy to remember to always choose your words wisely, but it certainly gets easier and easier the more you realize the importance of doing so.

Even with the abundant feeling of having 54 hours, I wasn't blind to the fact that I had to fit in sleeping, eating, working, spending time with family, etc. So I immediately got to work.

I could feel myself getting nervous trying to think about what I was going to talk about to a group of 40+ homeless individuals. This was outside my realm of comfort, but I've recognized nervousness as a good thing.

Since I didn't have a lot of time to prepare, I needed to give myself some grace, knowing I would make mistakes. With that in mind, I walked through those seven principles one by one before I even determined my topic.

1. Running away from my fears actually makes things worse.

2. The only mistake is not trying.

3. It is okay to be nervous.

4. Give yourself permission to suck.

5. It is not about you.

6. Tell a story.

7. Know your audience is human.

Number one I've already checked off along with number two since I accepted the opportunity to speak. I wasn't going to run away nor was I going to not try. Number three I've read a thousand times, but it still helps calm me down knowing it is okay to be nervous.

I took some time on number four to give myself permission to suck. Since I've read this over and over before, it would be easy to skip it and move on, but I know it's important to continue to remind myself that it is more than okay to make mistakes because, otherwise, I would never learn anything and I wouldn't grow.

Number five, it is not about you, helped put the opportunity to speak into perspective. In the end, this isn't about me or my fears. It's about serving my audience. My audience Tuesday night would be a crowd of homeless people who are at a low point in their lives. I wanted to add value to their lives whether that's distracting them from something that's been bringing them grief, giving them an uplifting message, or sharing the love of God with them for the first time.

Number six is key in these situations. I would have to tell a story that I'm already familiar with, so I wouldn't have to learn a whole bunch of new content in a short period of time. When you don't have a lot of time to prepare, stick with what you know. The leader of the trip to the homeless shelter had given me free reign to talk about whatever I wanted, so a story from the Bible that I knew well would work best.

Last, but not least, I knew my audience was comprised of humans. I don't care if my audience members are made up of the homeless or business executives; they are all human. Humans that can feel the fears and passions of others. They have their own set of fears, insecurities, and faults. Most importantly, humans forget. Even if

I just completely bombed on stage, I might as well have *Men in Black* amnesia technology because by morning most, if not everyone, would have forgotten about me or any mistakes I made. The only one who would truly remember my performance was me and me alone.

Going through that put my nerves and fears in check. My coward self was silent for the most part, and I was ready to get started.

I took the rest of the day to pinpoint what Bible story I could use to help a group of homeless people who are down on their luck. Trying to come from their point of view, I chose the story of Job.

Tuesday came so fast, but I had prepared and was ready regardless of how my fears made me feel.

I started strong, but when I got to the point where Job loses all of his children. I said, "If I ever got the news my child died . . ." I looked back at my wife and our daughter, Nella, and then looked back to my audience and said, "I'll show you a broken man." As I started to cry, feeling the anguish, I struggled a bit to recover.

Once I grabbed a hold of myself, I continued the story. When I noticed a lady in the front tearing up from the message, I felt reaffirmed that this wasn't about me, and I had a higher purpose for speaking.

I finished the story and tied in my message. I thanked them for listening, and they applauded as I made my way back to my seat. Another staff member closed the evening with prayer.

Afterwards, that woman who cried during my speech approached my wife and told her story. Her life had spiraled out of control very similar to Job's life. She had recently lost everything. Her father,

her husband, and her child had all passed away in a matter of a few months.

She was now homeless and had emotionally hit rock bottom. She told my wife she was losing faith in God, but the message I gave that night gave her a new hope. They both cried together as my wife prayed over her. That night was truly not about me, and her story made that point even more real.

I left Beacon Light Mission that night feeling more alive just like I do after every speech or talk. I realized if I hadn't taken the time and committed to controlling my fears, I would never have agreed to speak that night. I had grown a lot since high school, and I couldn't wait to speak again. Speaking has now become a thrill to me, and something I look forward to.

CHAPTER 29

MINI MENTOR

The purpose of this book is really to help you overcome your fear of public speaking rather than turn you into a well-polished speaker/presenter. There are thousands of topics we could cover for further improvements, but those are well beyond the scope of this book.

You can easily find resources ranging on topics from engaging your audience to choosing an appropriate tone for your message. There are books, videos, and coaching available to you at a low cost or most of the time for free. I certainly encourage you to seek them out if you really want to take your speaking ability to the next level.

To help me improve, I pick a particular speaker and dive deep into his/her work for 30 days. I read their books, watch their videos on YouTube, follow them on twitter, and find out what I can learn from them. At the end of the 30 days, I take what I've learned from them and make a plan to put those lessons into practice. Additionally, I contact them (preferably after leaving them a review), thank them for sharing their knowledge and expertise, and ask if they have any nugget of advice for the speech I will be giving next week.

By diving deep into various speakers, I gain mentors I can learn from. You can do this not just with public speaking, but with any topic to learn from and connect with experts in any field.

Not everyone responds, but those who have responded have always shared priceless words of wisdom from their experiences.

One person I reached out to who I truly respect and admire is Patrick King, a Social Interaction Specialist and author of *Fearless Public Speaking* (and many other books). I studied his work during one of my 30 day deep dives. After reading several of his books, I reached out to him on his website. He responded and gave me a piece of advice for a humorous speech competition I had coming up. His advice reiterated the importance of filming ourselves to get feedback and studying others who we would like to imitate.

I film myself quite often as it is, but after hearing that advice again from Patrick, I filmed everything leading up to the competition. I watched the recordings of myself so much it almost felt like stalking, but I improved by getting the audiences' point of view. Incorporating that feedback into my speech helped me win various levels of a Toastmasters competition. While I didn't win at the district level, I progressed so much from the feedback my recordings gave me.

—Cody's Note—

If you would like to know more about Patrick King, you can go to his website www.patrickkingconsulting.com or you can go on www.amazon.com and check out some of his books. —And no I don't make any money from you going to either of those sites ☺.

CHAPTER 30

CONCLUSION OF THIS BOOK— THE BEGINNING OF YOUR JOURNEY

Have we been on a journey or what? Bravo to you for making it to the finish line. Of course, this is just the finish line of the book. You are now at the beginning of your journey to become a courageous speaker. I hope by now you have already taken your first step(s) to put what you've learned into action.

You've learned how to distinguish between the coward in you and the stage fighter in you. You understand that you put limits on yourself, and it's up to you to bust through them. You know that discipline is the push to take the first step and courage is the pull to make the next step even easier.

Most of all, you know whom to punch in the face and how to do it. You are incredible, and you are capable of more than you can imagine. Stage Fight brothers and sisters UNITE!

ABOUT CODY SMITH

Cody Smith is passionate about the power of public speaking, and even more passionate about teaching & coaching others to punch their own fears in the face. Cody's mission is to give people actionable steps to quickly become courageous speakers.

When he's not speaking, coaching, or writing he loves:

- Eating cheesecake

- Throwing boomerangs

- Trying to *catch* boomerangs

- Playing with his 1 year old (which is like playing with a smaller, smarter version of himself)

- Hosting fake job interviews with random strangers inside elevators

- Not speaking in third person about himself

Cody currently lives in Southern California and is crushing several new writing projects waiting to be published.

You can connect with Cody via email:

Cody@stagefightclub.com

COURAGEOUS SPEAKER COACHING PROGRAM WITH CODY SMITH

There are a thousand and one ways to get from A to B. Some are faster than others. With speed comes saving life's most limited resource: time—which waits for no one.

Sprinting from A to B without a map or on a familiar route can lead to getting nowhere fast unless you have the support and guidance from someone whose has already trail blazed that path who can show you the ropes.

Put fuel to the fire on your journey to become a courageous speaker by hiring a coach and mentor. Hiring me as a coach will put you on the path of the straight and narrow as we collaborate together to identify your fears, address your key areas to see the most improvement in the fastest amount of time, and add a critical dose of accountability and mentorship to bring your public speaking to the next level and beyond.

Decide to work with me and commit to conquering your fears of public speaking, you will:

- Pinpoint limiting beliefs, negative affirmations, and thought patterns that are preventing you from reaching your goals

- Develop custom tailored plan to face your fears public speaking on a weekly basis

- Get advice and guidance from someone who has truly walked a mile (or two) in your shoes

- Receive priceless feedback on your speeches each and every week to super charge your speaking improvement

- Get the accountability you need to stick to your custom plan

- Build lasting confidence to speak in front of an audience even when you are afraid

- Learn tried and true strategies to punch your fears in the face!

If you are beyond seriously about becoming a courageous speaker than contact me at Cody@stagefightclub.com and we'll see if you are a good fit for the Courageous Speaker Coaching Program.

REQUEST FOR A REVIEW

What did you think about Stage Fight?

First and foremost, thank you purchasing Stage Fight and making it literally to the end of this book. Out of all the books at your disposal you chose this one and I am forever thankful. You invested your time and energy into getting this far, and I hope, beyond a shadow of a doubt, it was time and energy well spent.

If you enjoyed the book, can you do me a fist-bump solid? Please submit a review of Stage Fight on Amazon. This allows other to-be courageous speakers more easily find this book, and also helps me refine and hone my writing to improve this and all future writing projects to come.

As always, you can reach me at Cody@stagefightclub.com.

All the best to you and your journey,

Cody Smith.

SPEAKING REQUEST

Could your group, organization, or corporation benefit by going beyond the content of this book to dominate the fear of public speaking to vastly improve the confidence and communication of your team?

Are you interested in contacting Cody for:

- A Stage Fight workshop for your workplace full of public speaking fear punching and courage building to boot

- Speaking engagements on conquering the fear of public speaking

To invite Cody to speak at your next event, get in touch with him directly through his website's contact form at http://www.stagefightclub.com/contact

Or by email: Cody@stagefightclub.com

Made in the USA
Columbia, SC
10 February 2019